SMALL FARM AGRICULTURE IN SOUTHERN EUROPE

Small Farm Agriculture in Southern Europe

CAP reform and structural change

Edited by
ERIC MONKE
Agricultural and Resource Economics
The University of Arizona
Tucson, Arizona

FRANCISCO AVILLEZ
Universidade Technica de Lisboa
Lisboa, Portugal

SCOTT PEARSON
Stanford University
Stanford, California

Research coordinated by
FRANCISCO AVILLEZ
Instituto Superior de Agronomia
Universidade Technica de Lisboa
Lisboa, Portugal

GAETANO MARENCO
Centro di Specializzazione e Ricerche Economico-Agrarie per il Mezzogiorno
Portico, Italy

CARLO PERONE-PACIFICO
Dipartimento di Economia Agroforestale e dell'Ambiente Rurale
Universita della Tuscia
Viterbo, Italy

Routledge
Taylor & Francis Group

LONDON AND NEW YORK

First published 1998 by Ashgate Publishing

Reissued 2018 by Routledge
2 Park Square, Milton Park, Abingdon, Oxon OX14 4RN
52 Vanderbilt Avenue, New York, NY 10017

Routledge is an imprint of the Taylor & Francis Group, an informa business

Publisher's Note
The publisher has gone to great lengths to ensure the quality of this reprint but points out that some imperfections in the original copies may be apparent.

Disclaimer
The publisher has made every effort to trace copyright holders and welcomes correspondence from those they have been unable to contact.

A Library of Congress record exists under LC control number: 98070984

ISBN 13: 978-1-138-34043-5 (hbk)
ISBN 13: 978-0-429-44065-6 (ebk)

Contents

Figures, tables and maps

List of contributors

Francisco Avillez is Professor Catedratico, Departamento de Economia Agraria e Sociologia Rural, Instituto Superior de Agronomia, Universidade Tecnica de Lisboa, Lisbon, Portugal.

Carlo Cafiero is a Doctoral student, Department of Agricultural and Natural Resource Economics, University of California, Berkeley, California, USA.

Antonio Cioffi is Professore Associato, CSREAM and Dipartimento di Economia e Politica Agraria, Universita di Napoli Federico II, Naples, Italy.

Joao Costa is in Gabinete do Planeamento e Politica Agro-alimentar, Ministerio da Agricultura, Lisbon, Portugal.

Paolo Cupo is Ricercatore, CSREAM and Dipartimento di Economia e Politica Agraria, Universita di Napoli Federico II, Naples, Italy.

Gabriele Dono is Assistant Professor, Dipartimento di Economia Agroforestale e dell'Ambiente Rurale, Universit` degli Studi della Tuscia, Viterbo, Italy.

Hugo Ferreira is in Gabinete do Planeamento e Politica Agro-alimentar, Ministerio da Agricultura, Lisbon, Portugal.

Joao Jesus is an Economist, AGROGES Consultants, Lisbon, Portugal.

Manuela Jorge is an Economist, AGROGES Consultants, Lisbon, Portugal.

Gaetano Marenco is Professore Ordinario and Head, CSREAM and Dipartimento di Economia e Politica Agraria, Universita di Napoli Federico II, Naples, Italy.

Eric Monke is Professor, Department of Agricultural and Resource Economics, University of Arizona, Tucson, Arizona, USA.

Scott Pearson is Professor, Stanford University, Stanford, California, USA.

Carlo Perone-Pacifico is Professor and Dean of the Facolt` di Scienze Agrarie, Dipartimento di Economia Agroforestale e dell'Ambiente Rurale, Universit` degli Studi della Tuscia, Viterbo, Italy.

Eugenio Pomarici is Ricercatore, CSREAM and Dipartimento di Economia e Politica Agraria, Universita di Napoli Federico II, Naples, Italy.

Fabrizio Sallusti is a Postdoctorate researcher, CSREAM and Dipartimento di Economia e Politica Agraria, Universita di Napoli Federico II, Naples, Italy.

Simone Severini is Assistant Professor, Dipartimento di Economia Agroforestale e dell'Ambiente Rurale, Universit` degli Studi della Tuscia, Viterbo, Italy.

Alessandro Sorrentino is Assistant Professor, Dipartimento di Economia Agroforestale e dell'Ambiente Rurale, Universit` degli Studi della Tuscia, Viterbo, Italy.

Carlos Trindade is an Economist, AGROGES Consultants, Lisbon, Portugal.

Preface

This book presents the results of a research project undertaken in the early and mid- 1990s about small farm agriculture in Portugal and Italy and the likely impacts of CAP reform. Several years later, the full implications of that reform have yet to be felt. Small farm agriculture has changed little from that reported in this research. Such stagnation is in part a consequence of unusually favorable markets for most commodities and partly the result of somewhat sluggish performances in the national economies. The results and projections presented in this book thus remain timely and relevant to the evolution of small farm agriculture in the next century.

We owe thanks to a great many institutions and individuals for their assistance. This research was supported by the European Economic Community under Research contract number 8001-CT91-0302. Government institutions were helpful at numerous junctures. Particular mention should be made of the Farm Accounting Data Network and the national ministries of agriculture. Various producer organizations were also helpful in collecting and interpreting data about small farm agriculture. We owe thanks also for the advice and insights of many academic economists; particular mention should be made of Tim Josling, Stefan Tangermann, and Michele de Benedictis. Any failings or inaccuracies that remain are entirely our responsibility.

For the preparation of this manuscript, we owe great thanks to Pat Olsson of the Department of Agricultural and Resource Economics at the University of Arizona. Linda Taber, of the same department, provided much assistance with graphics and maps. Finally, we owe special gratitude to our many friends in Palo Alto, California and Lago di Vico, Italy. They made the writing of this manuscript more than a pleasure.

Tucson, Arizona
January, 1998

1 Introduction

Francisco Avillez and Eric Monke

Small farm agriculture was once considered to be little more than an anachronism of the development process. Large farms were expected to be the end result of successful economic development, because farmers could take advantage of economies of scale, capital intensification, and larger land areas to increase labor returns to levels commensurate with those of the industrial and service sectors. Meanwhile, this process would release other labor from the drudgery of farming to pursue more lucrative, and often more exciting, opportunities in the cities. Agriculture would be left to the efforts of a few large operators.

Today, views in Europe are quite different. Increases in per capita incomes have been very large, but small farms have proven to be a durable part of the agricultural landscape. Outmigration of agricultural labor has been substantial in all countries, particularly in the decades after World War II. Outmigration has continued in recent years, and the total labor force in agriculture has declined markedly. By the early 1990s, agriculture accounted for less than 10 percent of the labor force in the EC12; in the EC9 (excluding Portugal, Spain and Greece), the share was less than 5 percent (Folmer et al., 1995).

The number of farms continues to decline, allowing steady increases in numbers of larger farms. But the shifts among size classes in the shares of farm numbers have been surprisingly small. The largest size class of farms (>50 hectares (ha)) accounts for about 10 percent of farm numbers and about half of cultivated area. These shares have remained stable over recent decades (Folmer et al., 1995). A substantial group of small farms has remained. In the 1990s, about 85 percent of farms in the EC12 are smaller than 20 ha. Even in the EC9, farms between 5 and 50 ha accounted for half of farms and nearly as large a share of total area. Shares of small farms in total numbers are highest in the southern countries. In Italy and Portugal, for example, the proportion of small farms in farm numbers exceeds 95 percent. Small farms account for a much smaller share of agricultural area than of farm numbers. But their prominence remains unmistakable to even the most casual observer of agriculture.

1

The small farm now is viewed increasingly as a viable economic unit. Certainly, agronomic considerations affect the potential for small farms to compete against their larger counterparts. But for at least some crops, most available economies of scale can be attained on farms that are relatively small. The option for farmers desiring change then is not merely to grow large or liquidate assets and flee the sector. Instead, farmers can choose to change their small farms, remain in rural areas, and find additional employment off the farm.

The concern for these individuals is not just the rate of return to their labor, but also the total income they can garner from a relatively small farm. A variety of family employment strategies has emerged-some with family members working in full-time jobs outside the farm and part-time jobs on the farm, others with different family members specializing between farm and off-farm employment.

The small farm has gained increased status within policy circles as well, particularly among those who find undesirable the prospect of further urban growth and increased depopulation of rural areas. Both changes can bring onerous effects. Urban problems of crime, poor public services, and environmental degradation become more difficult to control, while rural areas become increasingly backward and isolated from the economy and society. Small farms, part-time farming, and provision of attractive employment opportunities complementary to agricultural activities play major roles in most plans for rural development and rural industrialization.

Two opposing views of small farm agriculture have emerged. In one, small farms are hopelessly backward vestiges of the development process. In the other, small farms are poised to play a role in economic growth and remain a durable part of the rural landscape. Both perspectives have merit in analyzing prospects for agricultural transformation.

Small farms are diverse, and farms have remained small for a number of reasons. Traditional farms, usually managed by older or less mobile individuals, are often unable to leave the sector. For these farms, land ownership at least guarantees a reliable supply of food and income, however meager. Transfer policies to subsidize incomes have assisted the survival of such lifestyles, particularly in Italy. Macroeconomic and land market policies also have contributed to hesitancy to sell land and leave the sector. Periods of high rates of inflation and low real rates of interest on savings undoubtedly have discouraged the holding of financial assets and money. Land policies constrained the development of land markets. In Italy and Portugal, land rental and sales were limited by official price controls and restrictions on transactions. Justified with a rhetoric of protecting the small operator, this legislation also made exit from farming more difficult.

A second group of farms are those that have changed their farm operations in respects other than size. Some growth may have occurred, but usually not enough to make the farm a full-time operation. Policies of infrastructure investment and provision of services are critical to the success of a part-time farming lifestyle. But where rural areas could diversify successfully, small farms are capable of instituting substantial change. Advantages to holding the farm include also the value of housing and the value of owning a tangible asset, land.

The issue for analysts and planners is to assess the relative prominence of the two groups of farms and the possibilities for successful economic change. The issue became especially important in the 1990s, with the substantial reforms of markets and agricultural incentives. Policy makers expected support prices and export subsidies to be lowered substantially so that European farmers would become much more integrated with world market incentives. Recent events have not followed those expectations. Market prices have shown unexpected strength and remained above the levels of pre-reform support prices. In some countries, such as Italy, exchange rate depreciations relative to the ECU have raised commodity prices in domestic currency even further. But such events probably have only delayed eventual declines in prices. World markets are expected by most experts to resume their past trends toward ever-increasing supplies. EU production potential continues to increase, and this trend will intensify if eastern European countries accede to the European Union. Relatively high prices thus seem a temporary phenomenon, and farm incentives ultimately are likely to reflect the initial intentions of policy makers.

In the long run, policy makers need to identify the best ways to assist the process of structural change. At one extreme, policy makers could decide to support large farms and continued growth of the urban industrial and service sectors. Public investment resources would be spent on expanding urban services and the needs occasioned by continued urban population growth. Agricultural policy would focus on investments in infrastructure and commodity policies most needed by large farms. Adjustment assistance programs might be considered to retrain and relocate small farm families. At the other extreme, a strategy to support small farms would have quite different needs. Public investment would need to support services and infrastructure, but in a pattern that was more geographically dispersed. Agricultural policies and investments would be less focused on large farm interests and instead recognize that agronomic conditions do not always favor large farms. Policy makers then must consider returns to such projects as small farm irrigation. Competitive and fair access to policy measures would become important preconditions to an efficient agricultural policy.

Assessment of the competitive potential of small farms in southern Europe was the principal goal of a group of researchers from three universities in Portugal and Italy-the Instituto Superior de Agronomia (Lisbon, Portugal); the Universita della Tuscia (Viterbo, Italy), and the Centro di Specializzazione e Ricerche Economico-Agrarie per il Mezzogiorno (Portici, Italy). Economic analysis of small farm agriculture is used to develop a detailed portrait of current production and demographic patterns and to identify ways in which these systems might change. Particular attention is given to the effects of new crops, technologies, employment patterns, and policy directions that can sustain small farm systems in the new economic environment.

Three regions were selected for detailed study. Analysis in Portugal concentrated on the area near the coast, stretching (Maps 1.1 and 1.2) from Lisbon north to the Spanish border and covering roughly half of the country's width. This region has particular interest because it contains much of Portugal's industrial base as well as a substantial share of the value of agricultural output. In Italy, two regions were selected: the first considered some of the small farm zones of the south, concentrating on areas near Naples and stretching across to the eastern coast; a second area of focus comprised hilly rainfed zones north of Rome. In these areas, CAP-supported commodities, such as dairy and cereals, are prominent and relatively small farms dominate agricultural production.

3

Map 1.1 Study regions in Portugal

4

Map 1.2 Study regions in Italy

Detailed farm surveys were used to characterize small farm agriculture in each of the study areas. A data base was assembled to describe farm sizes, cropping patterns, production technologies, and demographic characteristics. Statistical techniques (principal components and cluster analyses) were used to identify homogeneous groups of the farm population. These groups are termed 'representative farms', and they serve as the analytical building blocks to study the impacts of changes in incentives and potential adjustments. Changes in incentives create pressures on Portuguese and Italian farmers to respond. The feasibility of those reactions - technological and crop mix changes, and structural adjustments - depends on the characteristics of the farming systems, the agro-climatic zones within which they operate, and the implementation of policy. Adjustment problems are most severe for zones with few alternative crops, farm structures with little room of maneuver for adjustment, and socio-economic zones with relatively inflexible factor markets.

The adjustment process is influenced also by the ways that Portuguese and Italian policy makers use the available EU and national policies that impact directly and indirectly on the agricultural sector. The use of existing policies and new initiatives in the socio-structural and agro-environmental areas depends not only on regional and farm characteristics, but also on the fund allocation decisions taken among the different zones and programs. Budgets always are constraining, and difficult choices need to be made both between agriculture and other sectors and within agriculture.

The farm models and information base was then used to evaluate policy change. The first task was to identify the expected changes in price policy and direct support resulting from the CAP reform and the GATT agreements and to develop projections of the relevant commodity prices, factor prices, and subsidies. These projections allowed the research team to construct a "projected baseline" of economic incentives. This baseline described the incentive structure for farming systems in the new EC environment after the MacSharry reforms, but without any adjustment in the farm systems. This result thus was useful to characterize the magnitude of the adjustment problem faced by the various farm systems.

Attention next turned to characterization of the potential for change. This prediction focused most closely on the possibilities to adjust crop mix and technologies and considered also the private and public investments needed to complement change. These adjustments were incorporated into the farm model to estimate the potential changes in incentives for each of the farming systems. The results demonstrated the impact of change on competitiveness and viability of the farm systems. Interest centered on structural change, differentiating between farms that appear destined to leave the sector and those that have economic potential to remain.

The book is organized into six chapters. The next chapter presents the methodological approach. The third, fourth, and fifth chapters describe the specific procedures used in each of the regions, summarizing the information collected and presenting the results. In chapter 6, the different regional results are compared from the point of view of future structural adjustment implications and policy options. This conclusion gives a comparative summary and provides a view of the potentials for future development.

2 Evaluation of small farm agriculture

Eric Monke, Francisco Avillez, Scott Pearson and Gaetano Marenco

Structural change of agriculture in countries such as Italy and Portugal has been rapid and striking. Population has left rural areas and agriculture in favor of urban areas and the industrial and service sectors. But this shift does not imply that the small farm sector is moribund. Desires to leave farming are heard often, but so too are discussions about which crops to plant and the adoption of new technologies and new investments - signs that some farmers plan to stay involved in agriculture.

For both farmers and analysts the key issue is how to distinguish between small farms that have the ability to compete in the agricultural sector and 'traditional' farms destined for extinction. The former group of farms becomes the foundation of the modern small farm sector; the latter provides the grist for the further growth of the farms that remain. Complicating the process of change are policies for economic and agricultural development. 'Rural development' and 'rural industrialization' are frequently heard phrases, and their implementation has important implications for the feasibility of various household employment strategies. Important also are the effects of agricultural support policies; many can favor either small or large farmers.

This chapter reviews arguments for the economic valuation of small farms - to identify whether farmers will have greater incentives to change or to emigrate. The first test of economic sustainability is competitiveness, comprising a comparison of farm returns with those available outside of farming. If non-agricultural employments represent the true alternatives for the labor and capital of farm families, the opportunity costs of farm resources have straightforward interpretations. Market wage rates and interest rates become the basis for opportunity cost measures. Prices from outside agriculture thus are used to value agricultural resources.

Because of the importance to farm families of total employment and total income as well as the rates of return to resources, consideration is given also to measures of total employment of small farm labor and capital resources. In the absence of total incomes that are comparable to those that can be earned outside

7

of farming, emigration from the sector will be likely and the process of structural change will continue (OECD, 1995). These results point to adjustment strategies of increased farm size and transition to competitive 'full-time' farms or to the attainment of rural off-farm employment and the establishment of 'part-time' farms. Information about labor requirements and cropping calendars is needed for assessment of the former strategy, and non-agricultural change and development strategies are critical to the feasibility of the latter approach.

The chapter reviews the approach applied in Portugal and Italy. Valuation becomes more complicated in the presence of divergences. Imperfections in factor markets and externalities can cause market prices to become inappropriate standards by which to judge small farm competitiveness. Although such imperfections are present in Italy and Portugal, these divergences usually are not large. Empirical estimation focuses on the identification and characterization of representative farms. The chapter also reviews the economic conditions that provided the background for agricultural incentives in the 1990s and the changes that are expected for the rest of the decade in the transition to the new CAP after adoption of the MacSharry reforms.

Competitiveness of small farms

Valuation of the economic performance of a farm system centers on its ability to offer an adequate return per unit of resource utilized. In the long run, these returns should be comparable to those that can be earned in alternative uses. If returns are less than could be earned elsewhere, pressures will arise for resources to be transferred out of the agricultural sector. Such transitions can be time consuming because of difficulties to sell assets and complications in separating the resources that are bundled together to enable farm production. So adjustment can require long time periods, involving generations rather than individual farmer decisions. But eventually, underpaid resources can be expected to leave.

Three indicators of farm system returns receive particular attention in this study. Long-run competitiveness looks at returns to farm labor after subtracting the full opportunity costs for each of the inputs used by the agricultural activity. Long-run viability measures the total employment offered by a farm system to see if the farm system alone can provide an annual income commensurate with incomes available off the farm; if not, off farm employment or expansion in farm size are needed to sustain the farm system. Short-run competitiveness considers owned land and capital as sunk inputs with zero cost and measures the rate of return to labor under these assumptions.

Long-run competitiveness

Long-run competitiveness measures the capability of a farming system to guarantee employed resources (and especially the labor supplied by the farm family) a rate of return comparable to the return to off-farm employment. This

8

indicator of competitiveness for a representative farm system is calculated from the net returns to farming per unit of family labor input. All other inputs (including hired labor) are fully costed. The calculation usually comprises estimates of the net profits of the farm, including the implicit returns to family labor as a part of profits. Dividing this amount by the input of family labor gives the return per unit of utilized labor.

A farm system able to pass the standard of long-run competitiveness offers returns to inputs at least as high as those offered at the margin by the rest of the economy. Moving resources out of agriculture in this circumstance would have the effect of lowering national income rather than increasing it. Competitive small farm systems thus contribute to economic growth rather than hinder it.

The attainment of a competitive level of returns is challenging for Portuguese and Italian small farms. Returns must be measured in a dynamic perspective because labor incomes in a growing economy are expected to rise over time. At the same time, prices for many agricultural commodities in Europe are expected to decline in real terms, often substantially. Much of the research in this project thus focused on changes that could be introduced to maintain the long-run status of competitive systems .

Long-run viability

Even if an activity offers adequate rates of return to inputs, it still may prove unattractive to economic agents. The decision by the operators of a particular farm system to remain a part of the agricultural landscape depends also on the total returns generated. A second measure of small farm competitiveness, therefore, considers the long-run viability of the farm and focuses on the total family employment offered by the farm system. Depending on the available family labor supply and the employment goals of the family members, farm systems may need to expand their size to generate acceptable total incomes. Even if the rate of return to labor is acceptable, the total return to labor could be too small to engender much interest in the farming activity. For such farms, increased land size or the attainment of complementary off-farm employment opportunities (part-time farming) are the only ways for the farm to remain viable. In most OECD countries, such strategies have been a major factor in enabling farm family incomes to maintain pace with the incomes of non-farm families (OECD, 1995). Because farm families tend to be larger than non-farm families, total family income for agriculture may be larger than that for non-agriculture. In Italy, for example, farm family household incomes are 45 percent larger than incomes of non-farm families (Folmer et al., 1995, p. 50).

Substantial attention is given in each of the regional studies to the data on employment, family size, and regional employment opportunities. Indicators of interest are the capacity to absorb labor surplus (CALS) and the degree of autonomy (DA). The CALS is measured as the returns to family labor, divided by the total quantity of available family labor. This measure shows the implicit average rate of remuneration of family labor. The measure assumes that all available labor desires to work and may underestimate the requirements of household activities and demands for leisure time instead of work. But attempts are made to adjust available labor units to compensate for age (young

9

and older family members are assumed to have less than a unit of available labor) and family obligations (women with children have less available labor).

The degree of autonomy (DA) shows the proportion of full time employment provided by the system. The DA measure can be used together with information on the time pattern of labor demands to assess the prospects of the system for expansion. When a system is competitive but utilizes less than one unit of family labor, the future viability of the system will depend on farm growth or off-farm employment to assure an adequate total remuneration to labor. Unless the laborer has a preference for leisure time, farms that are too small can give families an incentive to leave farming in favor of a full-time job.

When a farm system is competitive but employs family labor in a smaller quantity than is available, two alternative scenarios can be imagined. If the system will generate the income needed to assure a competitive return to all available labor, whether utilized or not, long run viability of the system seems assured. The family labor has no particular economic imperative to leave farming, and surplus labor can spend its time in the pursuit of leisure, rather than seeking off-farm work. These systems experience no great pressure for structural adjustment.

If the system does not have the capacity to compensate non-utilized family labor, the viability of the farm system becomes more problematic. Farm families are expected to seek increases in farm size or additional off-farm employment for at least part of the non-utilized family labor force. Such actions depend also on socio-cultural attitudes toward employment patterns within the family. But in either case, the comparative analysis of utilized and available family labor provides the basis for discussions of the dimension of the structural adjustment problem.

Short-run competitiveness

The final measure of competitiveness considers the short-run situation of a farm in transition. This calculation evaluates the incentives for a non-competitive system to remain in operation during a period when family owned resources are fixed on the farm. As an indicator of short-run competitiveness, this study estimates the return to all owned resources - owned land resources, management, family labor, and owned capital equipment (depreciation included) - per unit of utilized family labor. This definition of net returns to the farm system thus treats as sunk costs all inputs that arguably could be considered fixed. The measure shows the capability of the farm system to generate returns in the short run that are comparable to those earned by labor off the farm.

Economic conditions can be of crisis proportions when the measure of short-run competitiveness suggests implicit returns to farm labor that are less than the opportunity cost of labor. In this circumstance, agricultural labor would do better to abandon farming immediately. Such conditions give maximum encouragement to out-migration, and agriculture and rural areas would be expected to supply resources for a rapid structural transformation of the economy. If short-run returns are low for many of the farm systems, out-migration promises to challenge the capacity of urban areas to expand economic activity and to maintain social services and adequate living conditions. Critical policies for government become either expanded investment programs for urban infrastructure or expansion of programs to subsidize relatively poor rural areas and farm systems.

Market values and social values

Several complications arise to confound the empirical valuations of competitiveness and viability. Farmer access to factor markets of capital and labor often is far less than perfect, especially in small farm areas. Transactions costs and institutional rules can impede substantially the participation of farmers in these markets. When access to factor markets is limited, factor market prices outside of agriculture become only upper limits to the opportunity costs of family labor and capital resources (see Appendix). Farmers faced with limited access to factor markets may choose to spend their labor time or savings on agriculture instead of on leisure and consumption. Such choices reflect farm family preferences for work. The use of market prices to value farm family resources then overestimates the opportunity costs of family resources and underestimates competitiveness, with the magnitude of difference related directly to the extent of distortion of the factor market. If divergences are large, policies need to better integrate the farm sector with the rest of the economy.

Non-market externalities also might cause differences between economic value and market prices for factors. If positive externalities are associated with small farms, agricultural activity again is undervalued by market forces. But for the regions studied, nonagricultural values already are reflected in market values, particularly for land assets, because markets for recreation and non-agricultural experiences are well-developed. Additional arguments can be made for both positive and negative externalities, including contributions to national image and cultural values, adverse impacts of rural outmigration on urban areas, environmental degradation as a result of abandoning agricultural areas, and environmental degradation from farming (OECD, 1993).

But in the final accounting, the net value of divergences does not seem large enough to justify substantial subsidies to small farmers. Empirical estimates of externality values are not available, perhaps partly because such values are so difficult to measure (Portney et al., 1994; MacFadden, 1994). At any rate, public outcry has not been so large or irate to lead policy makers to believe that market equivalent values of such externalities are of large magnitude.

Domestic factor markets

In a perfectly competitive market with labor interested solely in maximizing incomes, the estimates of returns to farm labor can be compared directly with non-agricultural wage rates to evaluate competitiveness. If farm returns were lower than market wage rates, the farm system would be non-competitive and labor resources could be expected to leave farming for more lucrative employments. If farm returns are higher than those outside of agriculture, farmers are better off in agricultural production. Problems still may exist with

11

respect to the total amount of employment, but at least the rate of return to labor input is adequate.

If labor markets are less than perfect, comparisons of agricultural returns with off-farm wages can be too stringent. Imperfections in the labor market prevent farm labor from having easy access to non-farm jobs, and because of them the farmer is not able to offer labor services to the market at desired times or at acceptable wages. This situation is often present with industrial sector employment, where job schedules and employment numbers are determined in competitive environments that are less than perfect. In this situation, farm systems can offer marginal returns to labor less than market wage rates and still remain competitive. In this circumstance, the key issue for the farm family involves comparisons between farm returns and the implicit value of leisure time. Farmers may still be interested to work more off the farm. But because farmers have imperfect access to the non-agricultural labor market, they have no choice but to work more on their farms.

Similar results apply with respect to farm investment. Small farmers often have difficult conditions of access to capital markets; sometimes, they are thought to have strong aversion to debt. Policies may try to control interest rates and inadvertently create disincentives for banks to lend to small borrowers (Adams and Graham, 1981). In other situations, small farmers have high transactions costs to access formal credit, raising interest rates for borrowing well above the marginal rates of return to investment. Farmer decisions to self-finance investment thus may be taken somewhat independently of conditions in the formal capital market. The self-financed investment decision for the farm family considers the personal sacrifices of foregone consumption, and this opportunity cost can be less than the cost of borrowing on the formal capital market.

Some observers see apparent 'overinvestment' by small farmers, when in fact farmers are willing (and competitive) investors in their own farm. The implication is that market rates of interest can be too stringent a test against which to judge the economic health of small farms. Certainly, there are limits on the farmers' willingness to invest in their own farms. Some investments will be so large and costly as to preclude self-financing, and market rates of interest will be relevant. Most small farmers in Italy and Portugal have easy access to savings accounts, if not to borrowing. Returns on saving thus serve as a floor price for forgone consumption, and self-financed investment will not be entirely divorced from incentives in the capital market. Nevertheless, returns to self-financed investment for a competitive small farm sector can be somewhat below the market rate of interest for borrowing.

Measurement of opportunity costs of land is more straightforward. Land rental markets in most farming areas usually are dominated by agriculture, at least at the margin. Policies in Portugal and Italy have tried to distort market outcomes by controlling rental rates and biasing rental rights to favor tenants, especially with guarantees of long-term cultivation rights (Cory et al., 1993). But these regulations mainly have encouraged widespread avoidance of formal rental contracts. Distortions of rental markets were created as well, because landowners favored short-term leases and avoided longer term arrangements. Without long-term access, tenants were loathe to invest. Land still was widely available to farmers - at rental rates that were less easily known to inquisitive officials and researchers. But the opportunity costs of using farmland for one's own farm were well understood by all farmers.

Externalities

If positive externalities are associated with small farm agriculture, an argument can be made for subsidization of small farms to boost their competitiveness. Use of market prices will underestimate the social value of small farms. The provision of subsidies would boost net returns to farmers and make continued small farm activity more attractive. As policy makers have become more interested in sustaining rural populations and slowing rates of urbanization, questions have arisen about non-market values to rural activity and small farm agriculture (OECD, 1993).

Externality arguments fall into several categories. Rural areas and their populations are asserted to have particular environmental and cultural attributes that represent ideal national behavior and community values. However, linkage of these characteristics to economic values, and whether such values are externalities, is a tricky topic. Rural areas certainly may be an important part of the social fabric. But such importance is not a necessary reason for these areas to be subsidized by the rest of the economy. Indeed, analogous arguments with the opposite conclusion can be made, the attractions of the rural life provide a reason for rural people to accept returns to their labor that are less than those offered elsewhere in the economy. 'Rural areas as a national treasure' may be an important political argument in some areas, but the economic rationale is less than compelling.

A second externality sometimes asserted to justify subsidization of small farm agriculture is non-user benefit from small farm activity. Small farms help create an attractive countryside and contribute to the provision of recreational assets. Some consumers enjoy this environment without paying for it. Small farms are not able to capture their existence value from everyone who passes by the farm. Thus some positive externality value is present. But in most areas, these values will be reflected to some extent in market prices. Markets in Portugal and Italy to offer a 'rural experience' are well-developed. Facilities are found widely for agro-tourism; and land prices usually seem much above their capitalized agricultural values. As a result, land often will have a sales value much greater than its value in agricultural production. More isolated areas tend to reflect smaller nonagricultural values. Such patterns need not imply market failures, however, and instead reflect society's value for location. A pretty area that is not accessible and will never be 'experienced' by non-rural inhabitants has a value smaller than those of areas that are accessible. The valuation problem for areas that are not accessible may have some analogies to the famous question 'If a tree falls in the forest and no one is listening, does it make a sound?'

Negative externalities in the form of user costs arise in some rural areas because of the fragility of land environments. Erosion and destruction of the land resource base can arise from excessive or improper use of land. Other negative externalities involve the effects on the environment of nonfarm inputs, such as chemical fertilizers and pesticides. Some claim that these pollution problems have been encouraged by past CAP policies, particularly high prices, that have led to excessive runoff and accumulation in the environment. In these cases, solutions to the problems often involve less agricultural use rather than more, and small farms do not merit special support from policy makers. Instead, farms should be taxed to reflect the costs to land and water resources that are imposed by farming

A user cost that may justify positive support to rural areas involves externality effects of excessive urban development. Many have the opinion that urbanization rates are excessive, because rapid expansion of urban areas creates crime and urban pollution and compromises the quality of urban services, such as education, health, and sanitation. These externality costs arise from a failure to accommodate fully the process of structural change, and they reflect some of the frustrations, limitations, and inconsistencies of policy makers in dealing with change. In urban areas, change is thought to be occurring too fast for policy to keep pace. In rural areas, rates of economic adjustment are thought to be too slow, leaving resources stuck to earn rewards that lag well behind those in the rest of the economy.

The hard part of structural adjustment policy is to find the right balance between these two tendencies and to identify the optimum rate of movement of resources from rural to urban areas. Such calculations usually are well beyond the capability of policy makers and social scientists. An often appealing way for policy makers to resolve these conflicts is for rural people to enjoy higher returns without relocation to urban areas - hence the attraction of development strategies with rural development emphases. But urban user cost arguments by themselves would seem to offer little justification for explicit subsidies to rural living. Instead, policy makers need a better strategy of economic development to stimulate change in rural areas and a better anticipation of the effects of urban growth.

Externality arguments to justify special support of agriculture and rural areas stand on fairly thin ice. Rural areas offer particular opportunities to rural residents and unique benefits associated with the rural lifestyle. Because of these attributes, some rural residents may be willing to accept lower returns to their resources than are earned elsewhere in the economy. Similar arguments are made about the factor markets. Implicit returns to family labor and self-financed investment can be below market prices and still the economy can be said to be operating efficiently. In this instance, a direct comparison of agricultural returns with those earned outside of agriculture can be an overly stringent test of agricultural competitiveness and the sustainability of particular farming systems. Farmers may be willing to accept returns for their own resources that are somewhat lower than market levels.

There seems little justification for subsidized provision of resources to the rural sector. Market prices, or something reasonably close to market prices, represent relevant opportunity costs. For outside resources, the small farm sector should compete directly with other sectors and pay the higher opportunity costs needed to gain access to inputs from capital and labor markets. The key for the small farm sector is to have access to these markets, especially the capital market. Policies that focus on the cost of inputs rather than accessibility to markets may be misguided and bring negative consequences for small farms by reducing availability of resources.

The Portugal and Italy study

To assess the competitiveness of small farm agriculture and the implications for structural change, a research project was undertaken in 1993-94 in Portugal and Italy, in areas that had substantial small farm sectors and that at the same time experienced non-agricultural growth (see Maps 1 and 2). Areas distant from centers of non-agricultural activity or that were dominated by relatively large farms, such as the Po Valley of northern Italy or the Alentejo of southern Portugal, were excluded. The selection of zones was based mostly on secondary information and the personal knowledge of the research teams. The areas selected included, for Portugal, the coastal belt north of Lisbon. In Italy, two regions were chosen, one of hilly rainfed farms near the coast and north of Rome, and the other of areas located near Naples and stretching to the eastern coast.

After regions were chosen, the research focused on identification and characterization of representative farming systems. A farm sample was chosen, based on the national Farm Accounting Data Network (FADN). This network classified farms according to location, technical orientation, and physical size. The farm questionnaire used by FADN was elaborated to collect information specific to this study. These farm surveys were complemented by site surveys for each of the zones to collect information relevant to the representative farms, such as prices, the structure and conduct of markets, and off farm employment opportunities.

The information was organized into a data base for identification of the representative farms. These representations were based on cluster analysis of the farm characteristics; if this approach provided unconvincing characterizations of farm types, ad hoc estimations were applied. Regardless of the manner of identifying representative farms, the model defined structural, technological, and crop mix characteristics for each farm. The importance of each system within the study region was estimated by comparing characteristics of the representative farms, such as crop mix and farm size, with census data.

Economic valuation was based on technical coefficients, prices, and subsidies relevant to the crop and livestock budgets. These were introduced into the representative farm model to allow calculation of implicit returns to family labor and key indicators of competitiveness. These results were compared with the relevant opportunity costs for family labor. The latter values were chosen on the basis of secondary information and the results of field surveys. Even with ample fieldwork, estimations of the opportunity costs of labor were problematic. The enormous heterogeneity in labor ability and preferences for work and the large number of characteristics relevant to labor productivity (such as age, sex, level of education, and professional skills) cause great variation in the access to off-farm employment. General directions can be discerned in opportunity costs: older farmers have fewer alternative employment options than younger farmers; more educated farmers have a

15

greater range of options for alternative employment; and in some regions, employment opportunities are constrained by gender. But the variation in opportunity cost within the labor force was large.

Simplifying assumptions were made to arrive at measures that could be compared with estimates of agricultural returns. Male labor was used as the reference value for off-farm employment and wages. The age cohort between 35 and 40 was considered of particular interest, because at this age the farmer often must make a decision about leaving farming for off-farm work. This decision point seems particularly important for farmers with relatively low levels of education.

Baseline opportunity costs were represented by wages paid to unskilled workers. Higher wage rates apply to younger farmers and farmers with more education. These were taken from secondary sources, usually based on regional surveys of wages paid in various employment categories. Because of the difference between market prices and the values of farm family resources, farm systems were judged non-competitive only if their implicit returns were substantially less (usually about 20 percent) than market prices.

The structural adjustment implications of CAP reform are assessed on the basis of information about the degree of autonomy (DA) and the capacity to absorb the family labor surplus (CALS). Systems without future structural adjustment problems are the competitive and potentially competitive systems that appear viable for the long run. These systems provide an adequate level of income on an annual basis to meet the minimum employment needs of the farm family, even without off-farm employment. Systems with structural adjustment problems include the competitive and potentially competitive systems that offer low total employment relative to farm family availability and desired employment levels. These systems require an increase in farm size or improved access to off-farm employment opportunities if they are to remain a part of the agricultural sector. Potentially viable systems are those in which the labor surplus can be absorbed through farm size expansion or through increased off-farm employment. Non-viable systems do not offer this potential; constraints to expansion arise from net rates of return that are below market levels or technical factors, such as a cropping calendar that can not accommodate the labor surplus, or regional complications that limit farm expansion or off farm employment.

Classification of results

In considering competitiveness and viability, four categories of outcomes were of particular interest. The economically strongest systems were competitive systems that did not depend on direct supports from the reformed CAP. These systems needed no policy assistance, and market supply and demand relations offered adequate returns. The introduction of set-asides and compensatory payments makes subsidies of agriculture much more explicit than in the past, and the levels of such transparent subsidies are likely to be contentious issues. A second group of interest included competitive systems that depended on direct supports. These systems are perhaps the most vulnerable to changes in political sentiment. Systems that are competitive in the short-run but not in the long-run represent a third group - farms that can be expected to make a gradual transition out of agriculture. These systems are not competitive, but they are expected to remain a part of the agricultural sector until farmers replace their assets. This group of farms would be expected to disappear gradually, as owned capital is fully depreciated and as opportunities arise to liquidate land assets. A fourth group of systems are those that are not competitive by any measure. These systems present the greatest problem for structural adjustment, because they have the maximum incentive to leave the agricultural sector as soon as possible.

The farm system results are reported for two particular points in time. Interest first centered on calculation of the baseline year results to represent the situation in the early 1990s, the time of the empirical work and before the MacSharry reforms. Logistical reasons caused slight differences in the base years used in the two countries. The two Italian teams selected 1991-92 as the baseline year. Prices were relatively stable at this time, and macroeconomic policy had not yet implemented radical changes. The Portuguese team used 1992 as the baseline year - a time of relative stability and reliable data in Portugal.

To assess the initial impacts of the EC policy changes on farm incentives, the baseline results were re-estimated for full transition to the MacSharry reforms. Estimation of the projected baseline required projections of prices and subsidies that would prevail after CAP reform and the attainment of normal market conditions. Substantial depreciation of the lira and unexpectedly strong world markets caused Italian support prices for major commodities to increase in real terms after the MacSharry reforms, even though the reforms intended price decreases of as much as one third. In Portugal, negotiations have delayed the time of full harmonization until well after the MacSharry reforms were introduced. For these reasons, 'post-MacSharry' simulations do not have a definite date attached to them. But where time specification was needed, the year 2000 was chosen for the projected target of 'full accession'. By this time, prices were expected to have fallen to the levels envisioned when the MacSharry reforms were decided.

The projected baseline results were further modified under simulations of potential changes in crop mix and technologies. New crop and livestock budgets were constructed to characterize possible changes. All simulations were designed to satisfy three requirements - gradualism, consistency, and realism. Gradualism means that none of the potential changes could be so drastic as to obliterate the identity of the farming system in terms of size or product emphasis. Radical changes usually could be better analyzed as transformations from one system into another. When economies of size were present, different systems were identified within the same commodity group. Within each system, it thus seemed reasonable to assume constant returns to scale; non-competitive systems would remain non-competitive over the range of alternative sizes, until the system became large enough to take on the identity of another system. Some exceptions to this procedure were made when systems were allowed to become more specialized in their principal output. In these cases, the simulations considered changes in technology at the same time as changes in crop mix and the assumption of constant returns was not required.

17

Consistency means that the assumptions about institutional and market conditions were similar across the study areas. Each study gave similar treatment to the constraints of EU agricultural price and supply management policies, such as the maximum ceilings on subsidies, set-asides, dairy quotas, and the size of reference herds for beef and sheep. Each study group was sensitive also to the size of local markets and the possibilities of finding market outlets for locally marketed outputs. The stipulation of realism refers to the decision to analyze crop and technological changes that already were known in the regions and were thought to be adopted easily by the representative farmers. New research and development results could revolutionize agriculture relative to the changes analyzed here, but to foresee such change involves wishful thinking more than careful assessment of feasible actions.

Toward 2000: policy and price projections for Italy and Portugal

The initial projection of the baseline results involved recalculation of the returns to farming systems under the prices expected to prevail at the time of incorporation of the MacSharry reforms and the return of long-run conditions to agricultural markets. The prices required for the projected post-MacSharry baseline calculations include the commodity prices and subsidy programs stipulated under the CAP, prices for commodities outside of the CAP regime, prices for agricultural inputs, and prices for domestic factors - land, labor, and capital (Table 2.1). Many of the prices are affected as well by the exchange rate, because that parameter translates EU and externally determined prices into domestic currency. Attention thus is given also to expected changes in the exchange rate. Both countries experienced significant macroeconomic change in the early 1990s, requiring alterations of the domestic currencies during the period between the baseline and the projected post-MacSharry baseline.

The most significant influence on commodity prices derives from the implementation of CAP reform. In May 1992, after many years of negotiations to reduce the budgetary costs of agricultural policies, the EU Council of Ministers approved a radical reform of commodity market organizations (CMOs). The reform changed the level and the mechanism of financial support to farmers. For the major agricultural products, such as cereals and oilseeds, institutional prices were reduced by 35 percent and a system of direct payments per hectare was established. Farmers (except for small farmers) are obliged to set-aside 15 percent of their land to qualify for the direct payments; additional changes in production practices were mandated in the form of extensification and ecological programs. Analogous changes were introduced for livestock. Institutional prices were reduced and premium payments per head were introduced. These adjustments were consistent with the GATT agreements, reached at the end of 1993.

Global limits were established to limit potential expenditure for each commodity in each country. Base acreage and reference herds were set equal to their values in 1991. For each country, EC financial support cannot exceed a total expenditure calculated from the compensatory payment per unit (ha or animal) times the base acreage or the reference herd. In the initial years of

18

Table 2.1 Price change assumptions between baseline and Post-MacSharry estimates

Item	Portugal	Italy
	(percent)	
CAP Commodities	-35	-35
Non-CAP Commodities	-10	0
Inputs- Feeds	-35	-20
Inputs- Chemicals	-20	0
Inputs- Fertilizers		-8
Inputs- Seeds	-20	-8
Inputs- Fuel	-20	+16
Exchange Rate	-15	-15
		-22 (green rate)
Capital (percentage points)	-2	-0.7
Labor	+20	0
Land	0	0

Source: Team estimates

reform, the base can be set at the national or regional level, but eventually each country will have to establish bases at the farm level.

Additional changes in commodity markets, especially those for milk and horticultural crops, are associated with the implementation of the single market regulation. Agreements were reached in Brussels on the reduction of total milk production through the imposition of milk quotas. The application of EC directive 92/46 requires dairy farms to implement sanitary measures for milking, milk storage, and refrigeration. These regulations are intended to improve milk quality and will make difficult the survival of portable milking installations that are currently important in many of the sheep farm systems. In addition, all farms must introduce infrastructure to manage manure disposal.

Price projections differentiated between CAP and non-CAP commodities. For the commodities within the CAP regime (cereals, oilseeds, dairy, beef, sheep, and sugar) or indirectly affected by the CMO reforms (pork, poultry, and eggs), the Newport model was used (Josling and Tangermann, 1992). This model simulates the evolution of agricultural prices, taking into account the rules in the new CAP regulations and the GATT agreements. In each commodity market, the most constraining policy rules are assumed to dictate the commodity price. Usually, prices declined by about one-third relative to their levels of the early 1990s.

Price projections were more uncertain for the other commodities (fruits, vegetables, wine, and olive oil). The future of the CMOs for these groups remains highly uncertain. In some cases, differences remain between national prices and Common Market prices. Portuguese prices were assumed to be harmonized with European prices (because of the single market regulations) declining 10 percent from their baseline levels. When variety and quality differences cause the price for a given commodity to be different for the output of a particular farm system, prices are assumed to change in concert with the price of the standard variety. Relative prices for different qualities thus remain constant. Italian prices were assumed constant, because they are determined on large, national markets.

The CAP reform is expected to depress prices for some agricultural inputs, especially feeds, reflecting reduced demand and lower costs of raw material inputs associated with the lower CAP prices for cereals and oilseeds. Few empirical models are available to estimate the effects of CAP reform on prices of intermediate inputs - a partial exception being the MTM model (OECD, 1990) - forcing reliance on ad hoc assumptions about the evolution of prices. The assumptions for the Portugal study were that feed prices would follow the movements in cereal prices and that other intermediate inputs would decline by 20 percent by the time of long-run harmonization. The Italian studies identify four categories of intermediate inputs. Chemical and electricity prices are assumed to remain constant because agriculture plays only a minor role in price determination in these sectors. Fertilizer and seed prices are assumed to decline by 8 percent, reflecting the price depressing effect of declines in demand. These input markets should be much affected by the reduction in commodity prices and the introduction of the set-side programs. Feed prices are assumed to decline by 20 percent. Diesel fuel prices are expected to increase by 16 percent to reflect the removal in 1993 of the tax exemption for "green gasoline."

Exchange rate

Adjustment and incorporation of the new CAP policies has been further complicated for Portugal and Italy by macroeconomic instability. In both countries, the domestic currency experienced a real appreciation against the ECU before the baseline year that can not be sustained. These events require that the expected value of the domestic currency be adjusted in the calculation of the projected baseline. In both countries, substantial depreciation is expected to coincide with the transition to full accession. For the agricultural sectors, the depreciation will have beneficial effects from raising the domestic currency equivalents of ECU-denominated prices and subsidies. Macroeconomic adjustment thus will have the effect of moderating the disincentive effects of CAP reform.

In Portugal, the escudo began a sustained appreciation after 1989 and by 1992 had gained about 30 percent in real terms relative to the ECU. This tendency reflected a commitment by the government to maintain the nominal value of the escudo within the EMS. Because Portuguese inflation was higher than that in many other EC members, the escudo gradually became overvalued. Maintenance of the nominal value was easier in some years than in others; periods of economic recession and substantial increases in direct foreign investment eased the difficulty of defending the currency value. But substantial intervention also was needed on occasion. In 1989-91, the government made much use of official reserves ($US 14 billion) to maintain the escudo's value.

The historical experience suggests that some depreciation is likely in the escudo's value relative to its 1992 baseline value. Foreign direct investment and emigrant remittances are likely to increase with increased economic activity and improved access for Portuguese workers in Europe. Still, these movements were not considered strong enough to prevent some real depreciation. A depreciation of 15 percent for the projected baseline estimation was employed, reflecting an assumption that half of the appreciation since 1989 will be lost.

Italy's lira experienced pressures even more extreme than those encountered by the escudo. After 1986, the nominal value of the lira was held constant relative to the ECU. Italian inflation was relatively high, but high interest rates supported substantial capital inflows that helped sustain the lira's value. But by September 1992, the lira had become substantially overvalued. Attempts to maintain the nominal value of the lira within the EMS became unsustainable in the face of an economic recession and a rapidly growing public deficit. A strong speculative attack on the currency resulted in an exit of the lira from the EMS, and the lira depreciated against the ECU by more than 30 percent in a three-month period. The lira fluctuated around this value over the next two years.

The 30 percent depreciation in the real value of the lira seems an extreme reaction to the change in macroeconomic policy. Comparisons of inflation rates between Italy and its main trading partners over the 1987-91 period show Italian rates to be about 15 percent greater. The lira thus is assumed to be overvalued by 15 percent in the 1991 baseline estimation. This assumption is used in estimating the prices for the projected baseline.

Factor prices

Real interest rates are used in the farm models to evaluate the cost of working capital and the replacement costs of machinery, buildings, and other fixed inputs. The interest rate in both countries has been much affected by macroeconomic policy. Often, interest rates reflected the fiscal deficit and exchange rate policy instead of an underlying rate of return to investment. Prediction of the future value of the interest rate thus must be consistent with predictions of the value of the exchange rate and with expectations about fiscal policy.

In Portugal, interest rates were usually low or negative until 1987. Rates were high in nominal terms, but so was inflation. After 1987, interest rates were increased relative to inflation and have remained consistently positive in the range of six to nine percent in real terms. This regime of higher rates reflects the policy of the government to use the capital market as a primary means of controlling aggregate demand and limiting inflation. Inflation rates after 1987 were between 11 and 14 percent per year; annual inflation rates in the 1980-86 period were almost always in excess of 20 percent. Regulations were implemented, if somewhat erratically, to limit the quantity of lending for consumer durables.

The transition to a lower rate of inflation coincided also with a very substantial reduction in the relative size of the budget deficit. Measured as a percentage of gross domestic product, the deficit was cut to 4.8 percent in 1989 and has remained well within the single digit range since that time. This reduction was a dramatic change from the pre-1987 period, when deficits were between 10 and 15 percent of GDP.

The projected estimate for the real interest rate in Portugal is six percent. This estimate assumes that the government will keep deficits small and remain a relatively minor burden on the capital market. The projected rate is somewhat below the rate prevailing for the 1988-92 period. But it seems plausible for three reasons: foreign investment in Portugal should increase to equal or surpass its earlier levels, and emigrant remittances should continue to increase; higher incomes in Portugal will increase the supply of savings to the domestic capital market; and further harmonization of the EC capital markets will allow improved flows of funds among member countries. The potential for foreign exchange risk will continue to allow for margins between the real cost of capital in various member countries, but this is likely to be less in the future than at present.

Italian interest rates were much affected by exchange rate policy. Before 1992, the Italian government was committed to maintaining the nominal value of the lira within the EMS even though the government deficit was large. High interest rates were used to ensure inflows of foreign exchange and to control aggregate demand and inflation. After the exit of the lira from the EMS, interest rate policy became more flexible and Italy experienced a substantial reduction in interest rates. This change reflected the new freedoms for policy to fight recession and to reduce the public debt service burden. The discount rate, which had been as high as 15 percent in 1992, declined gradually to 7.5 percent in February 1994.

The real interest rate for the projected baseline is set at 2.8 percent. This projected rate is slightly lower than the 3.5 percent rate used in the 1991 baseline. This value is somewhat higher than the interest rates observed in many other European countries, but is consistent with the unusually large public debt in Italy.

Wage rate projections influence the estimated cost of hired labor and the opportunity costs of family labor. The heterogeneity of labor makes difficult the prediction of wage rates for each type of labor. The growth rates of wages for unskilled labor are likely to be different from those for skilled categories, and wages for women may change at rates different from those for men. The evolution depends on the growth of demands for each of the categories and is complicated further by changes in social attitudes toward labor participation. All of these render prediction of wage rates highly uncertain. The approach used here is to project the change in male wage rates and to assume that these changes are similar throughout the labor market.

The anticipated changes in wages are for more growth in Portugal than in Italy. This choice reflects the much lower income levels in Portugal and the expectation that Portugal will continue to narrow its income gap with the rest of Europe. Wage rates in Portugal showed essentially no growth in the first half of the 1980s. Legislation allowed large increases in nominal wages, but these were completely eroded by inflation. By 1985, real wages were essentially the same as they had been in 1980. After 1985, wages began a period of sustained and rapid increase, averaging four percent per year until 1990. After 1991, the increases moderated somewhat, because of the downturn in economic activity and increases in unemployment. Projections of future changes in wage rates assume an increase of about 20 percent over the remainder of the decade. Such rates are lower than those realized in recent years, but some slowdown in growth seems plausible as the income gap narrows between Portugal and the other EC countries.

For the Italian projections, labor costs are assumed to remain constant at their 1991 levels. The economic recession experienced in 1992 and 1993 and the slow recovery experienced in 1994 suggest that income growth by the year 2000 will be relatively modest. A second factor involves the agricultural labor market in Italy. Agricultural workers experience strong competition from foreign immigrant labor, and the prospects seem dim for increases in agricultural wage rates.

Land rental values are assumed constant in each of the countries. The substantial fall in many agricultural output prices should drive downward the land rental rates in each country. On the other hand, the compensatory payments should be capitalized into land values, exerting upward pressure on prices. The two effects should at least partially offset one another, promoting some stability in land values.

Conclusion

Market prices in the off farm factor markets provide an upper limit for estimates of the opportunity cost of family owned inputs and the long run competitiveness of small farms. On the one hand, farm family members may be forced to accept lower returns because their access to off-farm factor markets is constrained. The efficiency tradeoffs for farm families depend most immediately on the (unobservable) implicit values of family leisure time and foregone consumption. On the other hand, farmers may be willing to accept lower returns because of the attractions of a rural lifestyle. Such considerations are not thought to be significant in economic terms, however. The historical experience with structural change in Portugal and Italy indicates that labor will not accept large differences in returns between the agricultural and non-agricultural sectors. Comparisons with market prices thus serve as useful indicators of competitiveness.

Small farm agriculture is described with carefully collected data that describe the demographic characteristics, cropping patterns, and production technologies of small farm zones in Italy and Portugal. Statistical techniques and expert observation are used to classify and characterize the principal types of farms present in each region. The farms are then evaluated for the effects of the recent CAP reforms. Principal attention will be given to small farm adjustment problems and the prescription of the types of change that will be important to the continued economic survival of these farms.

Appendix to chapter 2

The opportunity costs of farm family resources

In conditions of perfect markets for domestic factors, individuals are expected to allocate their work efforts so as to equalize the marginal return to agricultural work, the wage rate available from off-farm work, and the marginal value of leisure time. These relations form the basis for a definition of efficient resource allocation by the farm family. This result can be shown with a simple household model. The household maximizes a utility function defined over commodities and leisure, subject to constraints of agricultural production technology, income and expenditure, and the availability of time.

$$\max \ U = U(c,m,l)$$

subject to:

agricultural production constraint $\ f = f(x_i,h)$

income-expenditure constraint $\ p(f-c)-p_ix_i + wn \geq qm$

time constraint $\ l + n + h = t$,

where u=household utility, c=consumption of home-produced agricultural goods, m=consumption of goods purchased on the market, l=leisure time, f=agricultural production function, x_i =agricultural inputs other than family labor, h=family labor used in agricultural production, p=price of agricultural output, p_i=prices of agricultural inputs, w=wage rate for non-farm work, n=family labor used in non-agricultural production, q=price of market goods, and t=total family labor time.

The constraints are straightforward, except perhaps for the second, that states that the cash income from farming plus the income from non-agricultural activity must equal or exceed expenditure.

The static optimum is found by forming the Lagrangean

$$\tilde{L} = u(c,m,l)+ \lambda\left[p(f-c)-p_ix_i + wn - qm\right]+ \gamma\left[t - l - n - h\right].$$

The first order conditions associated with the allocation of labor time are as follows:

$$\frac{\partial \tilde{L}}{\partial n} = \lambda w - \gamma \le 0, n \ge 0, n\left(\frac{\partial \tilde{L}}{\partial n}\right) = 0$$

$$\frac{\partial \tilde{L}}{\partial h} = \lambda p \frac{\partial f}{\partial h} - \gamma \le 0, h \le 0, h\left(\frac{\partial \tilde{L}}{\partial h}\right) = 0$$

$$\frac{\partial \tilde{L}}{\partial l} = \frac{\partial u}{\partial l} - \gamma \le 0, l \ge 0, l\left(\frac{\partial \tilde{L}}{\partial l}\right) = 0$$

These results imply that $w = \dfrac{(\partial u / \partial l)}{\lambda} = p\dfrac{\partial f}{\partial h}$. This is the allocation rule associated with perfect competition.

However, most small farm environments are characterized by less than perfect markets. In particular, employment opportunities and access to off-farm employment are not left purely to the market. Instead, policy and logistical considerations affect the timing and quantity available of non-farm (often industrial) work. To introduce the labor market distortion of a limitation on off-farm work, an additional time constraint is added to the model: $0 \le n \le N$.

The Lagrangean becomes

$$\tilde{L} = u(c,m,l) + \lambda\left[p(f - c) - p_i x_i + wn - qm\right]$$

$$+\gamma[t - l - n - h] + \mu[N - n]$$

The first order condition with respect to non-farm work becomes

$$\frac{\partial \tilde{L}}{\partial n} = \lambda w - \gamma - \mu \le 0, \quad 0 \le n \le N, \quad n\left(\frac{\partial \tilde{L}}{\partial n}\right) = 0.$$

If the constraint on off farm employment is binding, the farm family is left with an equi-marginal tradeoff between leisure and farm work. Both of these are less than the wage rate paid to non-farm work.

$$\frac{\partial u / \partial l}{\lambda} = p\frac{\partial f}{\partial h} = \frac{\gamma}{\lambda} \le w = \frac{\gamma + \mu}{\lambda}$$

The farm family would be willing to devote more time to off farm work, if such work were accessible. But off farm work often is limited by factory schedules, institutional limits on the length of work weeks, and overtime conditions. Workers thus find their off farm work activity limited. The decision for farmers then becomes whether to spend additional time working on their farms or to pursue other leisure. The optimum tradeoff is reflected in an equality between the implicit value of leisure time and the payoff to agricultural work.

Similar results occur for valuation of farm financed capital investment. In a perfect capital market, the opportunity cost of capital will be equal to the market rate of interest. But many small farm environments have less than perfect capital markets. Several factors - policy distortions, such as interest rate controls, high transactions costs for small farm loans, or debt aversion sentiments by small farmers - can cause capital markets in rural areas to be incompletely integrated with capital markets in the rest of the country. The result is that a farmer makes optimum investment decisions by comparing the return to farm investment with the implicit value of forgone consumption. This value will be less than the market price of capital.

The capital market version of the household model adopts the procedure of Iqbal (1986), extending the optimization horizon to two periods. The notation is changed slightly from the earlier model - subscripts 1 and 2 are used to represent the different time periods. Three additional variables are added: investment (i), external borrowing (eb), and self-financed investment (sf).

The basic two-period model is presented below:

$$\max \; u = u\left(c_1, c_2, m_1, m_2, l_1, l_2\right)$$

subject to an income-expenditure constraint in each of the periods:

$$p_1\left(f\left(k_1, x_{1i}\right) - c_1\right) - p_{1i} x_{1i} + wn + eb \geq qm_1 + i$$

$$p_2\left(f\left(k_2, x_{2i}\right) - c_2\right) - p_{2i} x_{2i} + wn \geq qm_2 + (1+r)eb$$

The last term $(1+r)eb$ represents loan repayment. Two identities relate the capital stock of the farm, investment, and financing:

$$k_1 + i = k_2$$
$$i = eb + sf$$

The first equation states that capital stock in the first period plus investment equals capital stock in the second period (ignoring depreciation). The second equation states that investment is financed by the sum of external borrowing and self-finance.

Substitution of these expressions into the income expenditure constraints allows formulation of the Lagrangean:

$$\widetilde{L} = u\left(c_1, c_2, m_1, m_2, l_1, l_2\right) +$$

$$\lambda_1\left[p_1\left(f\left(k_1, x_{1i}\right) - c_1\right) - p_{1i} x_{1i} - (eb + sf) + wn + eb - qm_1\right] +$$

$$\lambda_2\left[p_2\left(f\left(k_1 + eb + sf, x_{2i}\right) - c_2\right) - p_{2i} x_{2i} + wn - qm_2 - (1+r)eb\right]$$

The first order conditions of interest in the analysis are $\frac{\partial \widetilde{L}}{\partial eb}$ and $\frac{\partial \widetilde{L}}{\partial sf}$.

$$\frac{\partial \widetilde{L}}{\partial eb} = \left[-\lambda_1 + \lambda_1\right] + \lambda_2\left[p_2 \frac{\partial f}{\partial eb} - (1+r)\right] = 0$$

$$p_2 \frac{\partial f}{\partial eb} = 1 + r$$

The above relation shows that the marginal value product of externally financed investment equals the marginal cost of borrowing.

$$\frac{\partial \tilde{L}}{\partial sf} = \frac{\partial u}{\partial c_1}\frac{\partial c_1}{\partial sf} + \lambda_1\left[-p_1\frac{\partial c_1}{\partial sf} - 1\right] + \lambda_2\left[p_2\frac{\partial f}{\partial sf}\right] = 0 .$$

Since $p\frac{\partial c}{\partial sf} = -1$ (the value of increased self finance is equal to the value of the reduction in consumption), the previous first order condition can be simplified to the following:

$$p_2\frac{\partial f}{\partial sf} = \frac{\partial u/p_1\partial c_1}{\lambda_2}.$$

This relation shows that the marginal value of self financed investment equals the marginal value of first-period consumption divided by the Lagrangean multiplier, λ_2. But the marginal value of first period consumption is the Lagrangean multiplier for the first period, allowing the right hand side of the equation to be expressed as the ratio of two Lagrangean multipliers. To the farmer/consumer, the second period value will be equivalent to the value in the first period, discounted from the second period value by the consumer's rate of time preference, $1 + s$. Therefore, $p_2\dfrac{\partial f}{\partial sf} = 1 + s.$

The value marginal product of self financed investment equals 1 plus the rate of time preference. In a perfect capital market, the farmer is free to choose between self finance and borrowing, so that the marginal value product of both types of investment will be equal. Thus, $r=s$; the rate of time preference equals the marginal cost of borrowing (or the rate of return in the capital market).

Divergences are introduced into the model with two additional assumptions: external borrowing is assumed limited to some maximum, $\overline{eb}$; and use of the external credit market incurs transactions costs, $tr=tr(eb)$. Under these assumptions, the income expenditure constraints become:

$$p_1\big(f(k_1,x_{1i}) - c_1\big) - p_{1i}x_{1i} + wn + eb - tr(eb) \geq qm_1 + i$$

$$p_2\big(f(k_2,x_{2i}) - c_2\big) - p_{2i}x_{2i} + wn \geq qm_2 + (1+r)eb$$

In addition, a new constraint is created: $0 \leq eb \leq \overline{eb}$.
The Lagrangean becomes:

$$\tilde{L} = u(c_1,c_2,m_1,m_2,l_1,l_2) +$$

$$\lambda_1\big[p_1\big(f(k_1,x_{1i}) - c_1\big) - p_{1i}x_{1i} - (eb + sf) + wn + eb - tr(eb) - qm_1\big] +$$

$$\lambda_2\big[p_2\big(f(k_1 + eb + sf, x_{2i}) - c_2\big) - p_{2i}x_{2i} + wn - qm_2 - (1+r)eb\big]$$

$$+\mu\big(\overline{eb} - eb\big)$$

Now, the first order conditions become somewhat different from the perfectly competitive case:

$$\frac{\partial \tilde{L}}{\partial eb} = \left[-\lambda_1 + \lambda_1 - \lambda_1 \frac{\partial tr}{\partial eb}\right] + \lambda_2 \left[p_2 \frac{\partial f}{\partial eb} - (1+r)\right] - \mu = 0$$

$$p_2 \frac{\partial f}{\partial eb} = (1+r) + \frac{\lambda_1}{\lambda_2} \frac{\partial tr}{\partial eb} + \frac{\mu}{\lambda_2}$$

$$= (1+r) + (1+s) \frac{\partial tr}{\partial eb} + \frac{\mu}{\lambda_2}$$

The marginal value product of externally financed investment is equal to the marginal cost of borrowing plus the ratio of the marginal utility of income in the two periods (one plus the rate of time preference) times the marginal transactions costs of external borrowing, plus the marginal utility of external borrowing, converted to money by the marginal utility of second period income.

The first order condition with respect to self finance is unchanged from the previous case, i.e.,

$$\frac{\partial \tilde{L}}{\partial sf} = \frac{\partial u}{p_1 \partial c_1} \frac{p_1 \partial c_1}{\partial sf} + \lambda_1 \left[\frac{p_1 \partial c_1}{\partial sf} - 1\right] + \lambda_2 \left[p_2 \frac{\partial f}{\partial sf}\right] = 0,$$

$$p_2 \frac{\partial f}{\partial sf} = 1 + s.$$

Unlike the perfectly competitive case, the marginal rate of return to investment from external borrowing (as well as the cost of external borrowing) will now be greater than the marginal rate of return to investment from self finance unless the borrowing constraint is not binding. If the borrowing constraint is not binding, the multiplier μ is zero.

$$\frac{\partial \tilde{L}}{\partial \mu} = \overline{eb} - eb \geq 0, \quad \mu \geq 0, \quad \mu\left(\frac{\partial \tilde{L}}{\partial \mu}\right) = 0. \text{ But in general,}$$

$$p_2\left(\frac{\partial f}{\partial eb}\right) \rangle p_2\left(\frac{\partial f}{\partial sf}\right),$$

or $(1+r) + \frac{\mu}{\lambda_2} \rangle 1 + s.$

The presence of transactions costs for external borrowing also creates a wedge between the rate of time preference and the rate of return to borrowing:

$$(1+r) = (1+s) - (1+s) \frac{\partial tr}{\partial eb} = (1+s)\left[1 - \frac{\partial tr}{\partial eb}\right]$$

As in the earlier case of limitations on external borrowing, the rate of time preference of the farmer becomes less than the rate of return and the farmer makes investment decisions that are to some extent isolated from the incentives in the external capital market.

These results show that estimates of competitiveness must proceed carefully in evaluating the costs of domestic factor inputs provided by the family, especially labor and capital. Land can be valued more easily. Because the option for farmers is usually to rent out the land to other farmers, the opportunity cost estimation is straightforward. Agriculture use still is the alternative for land, only undertaken by different agriculturists. But for labor and self financed capital inputs, the alternatives for the family are leisure time and increased consumption. These values usually will not be exactly equal to observable market prices. They will be less, with the difference between market values for factors and implicit opportunity costs for family resources dependent on the extent of the divergence. These differences are not large in most developed country agriculture. But neither are they irrelevant. So long as imperfections and policy distortions are present in domestic factor markets, small farm agriculture can continue to demonstrate competitiveness, even though returns to inputs may be somewhat less than returns earned elsewhere in the economy.

3 Small farms in Northern and Central Portugal

Francisco Avillez, Manuela Jorge, Joao Jesus,
Carlos Trindade, Hugo Ferreira and Joao Costa

Portugal joined the EC at a relatively late date - 1986 was the year of formal accession, following just more than a decade after the Revolution of 1974. At the time of the Revolution, Portugal was still a relatively agrarian economy, but showed the signs of rapid structural transformation. In 1970, agriculture accounted for nearly a fifth of GDP; more than one-third of the population was employed in agriculture. By 1990, agriculture's share of GDP was only one tenth and the sector employed less than a fifth of the population (OECD, 1994). The economic transformation has continued through the 1990s. These shares remain well above those in Italy, suggestive of Portugal's considerably greater distance to travel in the structural transformation process.

Such declines have not much diminished the prominence of small farms. Small farms (less than 20 ha) still account for 95 percent of farms and 40 percent of cultivated area (Monke et al., 1993). Three regions account for most small farm agriculture in Portugal: the Entre Douro e Minho, Beira Litoral, and Oeste. Located on the western side of the country, north of Lisbon, these three regions are distinctive for the prominence of a small, fragmented, and very labor intensive agriculture. These areas also contain the country's most important urban centers, and population density is higher than in the rest of the country. The non-agricultural sector is very diversified, with ample opportunity for off farm employment. These regions thus offer a good opportunity to evaluate the competitiveness and long run viability of small farm agriculture, from both a part time and full time farming perspective.

Description of the regions

If CAP reform and the GATT agreement cause agricultural returns to fall below those offered by off farm employment of resources, out-migration from agriculture can be expected to accelerate. Adjustment will be quicker and easier for the zones closest to the coast because most off-farm employment opportunities are located there. Structural policies will be less critical there to ease adjustment burdens. For this reason, the research team differentiated the regions by degree of urbanization as well as the more obvious agricultural characteristics of agro-climatic conditions, pattern of production, and demographic patterns (Map 3.1).

The Entre Douro e Minho region was divided into three zones - the Litoral, the Intermediate, and the Mountain. Moving from the coastal zone (Litoral) to the interior, the geography changes from a plain to a series of steep river valleys to a higher altitude zone of rolling hills. As a consequence of this topography, agro-climatic conditions and patterns of production change from an intensively irrigated agriculture to one that gives more emphasis to livestock and forestry activities. Because most urban centers are located along the coast, the interior zones differ also in the demographic characteristics of farm families and the importance of off farm employment.

The Litoral zone is characterized by a gently rolling plain and land parcels that are the largest in the Minho, reflecting topography and cultural practice, in which inheritance customs (morgadio) long discouraged successive division of parcels. In areas closest to the urban center of Porto, the pressure from urbanization and the existence of many alternatives to agricultural activity have noticeable effects on the conduct of agriculture. Part-time farmers are prominent and horticultural crops are the most common outputs, intended principally for the Porto market. Other crops in this zone, of much less importance, include milk, maize, and kiwi fruit.

Further from Porto, but still in the Litoral zone, the importance of milk increases. Production usually is based on maize silage and annual forages. Production technologies are relatively modern. Although the zone is host to much industrial activity, an important part of the agricultural area is managed by full time farmers. Maize for grain and vineyards remain as important crops, continuing historical traditions. The importance of traditional crops has declined in recent years in favor of the more productive (for dairy) silage and forages.

The Intermediate zone is the most heterogeneous part of the Minho. The northern part of this zone represents the heart of high quality, vinho verde wine production. Except for an increased emphasis on white wine varieties instead of red, agricultural production patterns there have changed little in this century. The sector is dominated by mixed crop farms, with maize, wine grapes, and pastures for animals. The region has less urbanization and industry than the Litoral zone and offers few employment alternatives to agriculture. As a result, the zone has experienced substantial emigration during the last several decades. The farm population is relatively aged.

Incomes are relatively low and almost always supplemented by other sources, such as retirement pensions and emigrant remittances from other countries or regions of Portugal.

The central part of the Intermediate zone offers a sharp contrast to the north. In this area, substantial non-agricultural activity occurs, resulting in strong competition for labor. Part-time agriculture is the predominant form of agricultural activity. Competition for land resources is strong also, since the

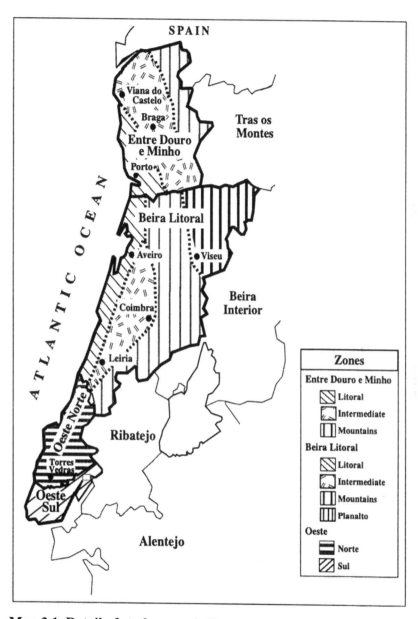

Map 3.1 Detail of study areas in Portugal

best quality soils are located in the more industrialized areas. Industrialization has made available financial capital for farm investment, and the rate of capital formation is noticeably higher than in more rural areas. The relatively modern and capital intensive farms are oriented to production of wine grapes and milk. The more traditional farms, still significant in number and in cultivated area of the central part of the zone, practice the diversified cropping pattern observed in the north; forest production is important in many of these farms as well.

In the southern part of the Intermediate zone, part-time agriculture dominates. Most farmers pursue traditional mixed cropping patterns. Milk is not important in this area, and animal production is instead oriented to meat. Labor markets have been integrated with the off-farm sector for a substantial period; transportation infrastructure is especially well-developed, facilitating travel to industrial employment opportunities.

In the Mountain zone, non-agricultural activity is modest. Emigration has been extremely important. The zone has a relatively high altitude, with less fertile soils and fewer opportunities for irrigation. Cattle production is the most important activity, based on extensive pasture systems, sometimes managed as common property resources. In the highest altitudes, cattle are replaced by sheep and goats. Forests, primarily pine and deciduous trees, occupy about half of the mountain zone. They play an important part in the local agriculture, providing firewood and bedding material for animals.

The Beira Litoral region is located south of the Entre Douro e Minho, also bordering the Atlantic Coast. The region is heterogeneous in topography, production patterns, and off-farm employment opportunities. Four zones were defined in this region - Litoral, Intermediate (Bairrada), Planalto, and Mountain (Serra).

The Litoral zone of Beira Litoral is a flat plain, often characterized by sandy soils, with a high degree of urbanization and a diversity of non-agricultural activities. In the northern part of this zone, horticulture and milk are the most important products, and part time farming is prominent. The center - the Vale do Mondego - has one of the country's most important irrigated perimeters. The government has invested heavily in irrigation facilities, drainage, and land consolidation. The principal crops are rice, maize, horticulture, and forages for milk and beef. Several types of agriculture are found in the southern part of the zone. Alluvial valleys contain fruit trees and irrigated cereals. Hillsides are devoted primarily to vineyards and fruit trees. The relatively mountainous areas are used for pastures and olive production. Throughout the zone, industrial production of pork and forestry are important.

In the intermediate zone, known as the Bairrada, the industrial sector has shown substantial growth in recent years. As a result, part time farming has increased in importance and now accounts for a substantial share of farms and cultivated area. Most farms are small, and the family is the only source of agricultural labor. Farm systems produce a diversified group of commodities, of which wine is the most important.

The Planalto zone is a relatively high altitude plain in the interior of the region. This area contains the Dao region, one of Portugal's most famous wine-producing areas. Vineyards have been declining in importance because of age problems. Within the zone are distinct sub-zones, differentiated by altitude.

In the lower elevations are found vineyards and apple orchards, cultivated by part time farmers. In the higher altitudes, off farm opportunities are scarce; emigration and general impoverishment characterize these areas. Pasture-based animal production, especially sheep (for milk and cheese), dominates production patterns. Farmers are relatively old and incomes are low.

The Serra zone is the most mountainous part of the Beira Litoral and consists of two discontinuous parts, one in the north central part of the region and the other located along the eastern border. This zone has the lowest incomes of any zones in the study. Non-agricultural activity is limited, and agricultural production is difficult because soils are poor. The land is dominated by old and low-yielding olive orchards, pastures for sheep, and pine forests. Emigration has been important in the past, with the usual consequences for the age structure and education level of the remaining population.

The Oeste region, located north of Lisbon, consists of a coastal strip of land and a mountainous area to the west (Sintra-Montejunto-Candeeiros). Two zones are important for agriculture. The Sul zone occupies the southeastern corner of the region, around Lisbon, and is characterized by poor soils. Farms are small and part-time, producing mainly cereals and pastures. The second zone, the Norte, borders the sea. This mountainous area contains numerous small valleys, often with ample water and good soils, producing wine grapes (although diminishing in importance) and horticultural crops (mainly potatoes, carrots, tomatoes, and lettuce). The latter crops are grown often with greenhouse facilities. Orchards of pears (pera Rocha) and apples are common, as are animal products - milk, beef, pork, and chicken. These products are intended primarily for the Lisbon market. Since accession to the EC, farmers have made a noticeable effort to modernize farms and marketing cooperatives, not always with better economic results.

Representative farming systems

The characterization of agricultural systems was based on interviews with selected farms from the RICA system. The sample of RICA farms was randomly selected on the basis of farm size and crop mix to capture the variation present in each of the regions. The sample size for the three regions was 240, distributed among the zones as follows:

Region	Zone	Sample
Entre Douro e Minho	Litoral	32
	Intermediate	34
	Mountain	31
Beira Litoral	Litoral	24
	Intermediate	22
	Planalto	23
	Mountain	24
Oeste	Norte	28
	Sul	22

35

Each of the farms completed a questionnaire developed by the project team and applied by the technical staff of the RICA service. Before application of the questionnaires at the farms, training sessions were held to explain the objectives of the study. Discussions made sure that all information requested was clearly understood and formulated in a manner appropriate to the farms and the zone under study.

The questionnaire requested three categories of information. The first part elaborated the farm structure and identified principal crops and technologies associated with each of the farm's parcels. Information then was collected about the principal restrictions and constraints to use of natural resources, especially water. The questionnaire also asked for detailed demographic information about the farm family, describing the age, sex, educational background, and employment histories of each member of the household. This information was then used to characterize agricultural production systems and the important constraints that affected each of the systems.

To analyze the information, a data base was constructed. The data base had four principal categories of information. The first module contained information about the farm family head, equipment, area, and technical orientation. The second module sought parcel-level information, linking information about crop selection, structural characteristics and constraints, potential areas for irrigation and drainage, and technology use. The third module was information about animal stocks. The fourth module contained the demographic information on all other family members. Particularly important information concerned the availability to work on the farm, opportunities to work outside the farm, and emigration experience.

Once the data bases were organized, representative agricultural systems were identified. The intent was to identify systems at a relatively disaggregated level. This allowed the team to characterize accurately farm structure and technology differences within each of the regions. To identify the systems, a cluster analysis was applied to the data. The systems identified by principal component analysis did not provide an intuitively attractive characterization of the different farm systems. Distinctions of crop and animal product specialization and farm sizes did not appear important in the cluster analysis. Yet, based on site visits, conversations with experts, and secondary information, team members felt confident that product mix and farm size characteristics provided a very useful way to characterize the important farm systems in each of the zones. A characterization in terms of commodity mix and farm size was not only intuitively plausible, but also would assist understanding the impacts of public interventions and EC policy changes. Many of these policies are defined in terms of commodity or size of the eligible farm. In the end, the team opted for a classification of farms based on direct observation of the data.

Four general characteristics were used to select and identify the systems: geographic location, production orientation, farm structure, and farm size. Farm results were arranged into relatively homogeneous groups and characterized by calculating the statistical properties of each of the main characteristics. In general, average sample values for the characteristics of the farm - area, number of parcels, crop and animal outputs, and so on - were chosen as

36

"representative." Representative farms were specified in terms of number and size of parcels, physical characteristics of the parcels, and ease and quality of access. Special attention was given to ensure that animal production of the model farm was consistent with crop production patterns and purchases of feeds by the farm.

Entre Douro e Minho farming systems

The information collected from a sample of 97 RICA farms allowed the research team to identify and characterize 11 representative farming systems for the Entre Douro e Minho region: 4 for the Litoral, 4 for the Intermediate, and 3 for the Mountain (Table 3.1).

Farming systems for the Litoral zone are oriented to the production of milk - the small, medium, and large dairies - and horticulture - the Litoral horticulture farming system. The three dairy systems are similar in crop mix. All emphasize irrigated forages and pastures; they consist of numerous parcels, many of them rented. Parcels are almost always close to the farm center. The average distance from farm to parcel ranges between 0.5 and 0.8 km for the three systems. Demographic characteristics are similar as well. Families have about 5 economically active members. All families have some participation in the off farm labor market, although to a lesser extent in the largest system. The average age of the head of household is between 40 and 50, and very few farmers have more than a primary level of formal education.

The main differences among the three dairy systems involve size and technology. Farm size varies from 4 to 14 ha, and the number of dairy cows varies from 6 in the small system to 36 in the large dairy. The higher carrying capacity of the large system reflects the use of higher yielding forages and greater specialization in milk production. All systems devote some area to the production of maize, potatoes, and vineyards. Much of this production is intended for home consumption, and its importance is relatively greater in the smaller systems. About 25 percent of total area in the small dairy is devoted to maize, potatoes, and vineyards, whereas the large dairy uses 90 percent of its area for forages and pastures. The larger systems also have more powerful machinery, more implements, and more developed technologies for milking. The small dairy uses a collective milking parlor, whereas the medium and large dairy systems operate their own parlors. Owned milking parlors have a lower incidence of disease.

The Litoral horticulture farming system is concentrated near the main urban centers, such as Porto. Farm size is about 2 ha, divided into 6 parcels, each located an average of 1.5 km from the farm center. More than 90 percent of the area is devoted to potatoes and vegetables, such as carrots, onions, and lettuce. As in all Litoral systems, irrigation is almost universal, and gravity fed systems dominate. Production is only partially mechanized. A tractor is used for plowing, but planting and harvesting are done by hand. In spite of its labor intensive production methods, only part of the available family labor is used. No labor is hired. The typical farmer is relatively young and has more education (secondary school) than farmers in the rest of the zone.

The representative farming systems for the Intermediate zone are oriented to the production of milk - the small and medium dairies - or wine - the small and medium wine systems. These farms tend to be even more fragmented than

Table 3.1
Entre Douro e Minho: main features of the farm systems

	Litoral				Intermediate					Mountain	
	Small dairy	Medium dairy	Large dairy	Veg-etable	Small dairy	Medium dairy	Small Vineyard	Medium Wine	Traditional	Small Sheep	Traditional Beef
Crop land (ha)	4.25	5.86	14.01	1.9	5.58	8.9	4.4	9.86	1.68	3.46	7.28
Forest area (ha)	0.58	3	3.52	0	1.18	1.24	2	4	2	1	1.35
Rented area (%)	40	33	49	7	30	58	51	0	24	13	40
Irrigable area (%)	100	99	96	92	98	92	62	21	83	100	24
Irrigated area (%)	89	88	96	92	98	92	62	21	83	72	22
Nº of plots	15	12	13	6	16	19	20	21	5	19	17
Average distance (Km)	0.53	.78	0.84	1.6	0.65	0.19	0.22	0.12	0.21	1.27	0.54
Prevalent activity											
Crops	Fodder crops	Fodder crops	Fodder crops	Horti-culture	Fodder crops	Fodder crops	Vineyard	Vineyard	Fodder crops	Pastures	Fodder crops
Livestock	Dairy cows	Dairy cows	Dairy cows	Meat cows	Dairy cows	Dairy cows	Dairy cows		Meat cows	Sheep & Goats	Meat cows
Forest	Pines	Mixed	Pines		Mixed	Pines	Pines	Pines	Mixed	Mixed	Mixed
Active family members:											
Off-farm employed FTE	1	1	0.2	0	0.5	0.3	1.9	0	0.3	0	0.3
On-farm employed:available FTE	2.80	3.40	3.00	2.40	2.70	5.20	1.60	1.20	3.40	2.00	3.50
utilized FTE	1.61	1.76	2.77	0.96	1.73	1.62	1.31	0.56	0.76	0.70	2.20

Source: Team survey

farms in the Litoral zone, largely because of geographical conditions. Average parcel numbers range from 16 to 21 for the systems. As in the Litoral zone, parcels are close to the farm center. Average distances are between 0.1 and 0.6 km.

Demographic characteristics show more variation among the farm systems than in the Litoral. The dairy systems have 5 or 6 active family members; the wine systems, between 2 and 4. Involvement in the off farm labor market is less extensive than in the Litoral zone, reflecting the lesser degree of industrialization. Dairy farms show a particularly large difference between available and utilized labor. Average age of the head of household is only 40 for the small dairy and between 55 and 58 for the other systems. Except for the medium wine system, farmers have little formal education.

The dairy systems are similar to those of the Litoral zone in terms of cropping patterns and carrying capacities. The small dairy has a herd of 9 cows on an area of 6 ha; about 75 percent of the area is used for forages and pastures. The medium system has 18 cows on 9 ha of cropped land; again, about 75 percent of the area is used for forages and pastures. Technologies show some differences. For example, the small dairy has a mobile milking parlor. But in most respects, the dairy systems are similar to those of the Litoral zone.

The wine systems are distinctive to the Intermediate zone. This zone is the heart of the vinho verde region, and production of these wines has long occupied a central role in the region's agriculture. In recent years, growth of external demand has encouraged much expansion in production of white wines. The Intermediate small wine system is the more traditional system. It has an area of 4.4 ha. About 30 percent of the area is used for vineyards of vinho verde (red and white). The remaining area is used for maize, potatoes, and forages for milk and beef production. The farm is partly mechanized and grapes are divided between the cooperative and home processing.

The recent growth in wine markets and changes in production patterns are represented by the Intermediate medium wine system. This system has an area of 10 ha. About 55 percent of the land is used for vinho verde vineyards (mainly white); maize, potatoes, and fruit trees are grown on the remaining area. This system is more mechanized than the smaller systems, and most grapes are processed by the cooperative. Demographic characteristics of this farm system are distinctive. The family has 1.2 units of available labor, all utilized and accounting for only half of the total labor needed by the farm. Important hired labor inputs involve mainly harvesting and pruning. The farmer is male, average age is 57, and the education level is high.

The Mountain zone systems are the lowest income farms in the region. Farms tend to be small and highly fragmented. Irrigation is common on most farms, but less so than in the litoral and intermediate systems. Farmers have few alternatives to on farm employment, and differences between available and utilized labor are large in many of the systems. Farmers are between 40 and 50 years old, with little education.

Three systems characterize mountain zone agriculture. The mountain diversified system has an area of 1.7 ha. About 75 percent of the area is used for forages and pasture to feed 2 dairy cows and 1 male animal. Maize, oats, and potatoes are the remaining crops. Mechanization levels are low and the cow is milked by hand. The sheep and goats system has an area of 7.3 ha. More than half of the area is used for forages and pastures; maize, beans, and potatoes are the other dominant crops. The level of mechanization is low. The beef system also has an area of 7.3 ha. About 70 percent of the area is used for forages and pastures. Maize, potatoes, vineyards, and orchards are the other crops.

Beira Litoral farming systems

Eleven representative farms were developed for the Beira Litoral, based on the results of a sample survey of 93 RICA farms: 5 for the Litoral, 1 for the Intermediate (Bairrada), 3 for the Planalto, and 2 for the Mountain zone (Table 3.2). Except for the horticultural system of the Litoral zone, farms tend to be slightly larger than farms of the EDM. Off farm employment opportunities are more limited, and the participation rate of farm families in the non-farm labor market is much smaller than in the Minho. Most farm systems have substantially more labor available than is utilized. The average age of the household head is usually between 40 and 60, with little formal education.

Litoral farms show large differences in size and product orientation. The more traditional systems are represented by medium dairy and an olive-wine system. These farms are not much different from farms found in the Minho. Each system has a size of 7 or 8 ha, divided into 10 or 11 parcels. The dairy system maintains a herd of 14 cows and is oriented to the production of forages and maize. The farm is highly mechanized and has its own milking parlor. The olive and wine system has a relatively small proportion of irrigated land (40 percent), accounting for its production orientation. About two-thirds of the area is used for olives and vineyards, with horticulture and maize accounting for most of the remainder.

More distinctive are the small horticultural farm, the specialized fruit system, and the rice system. The small horticultural farm has 1.2 ha, divided into 5 plots. About 70 percent of the land is devoted to carrots, green peas, and green beans. This crop selection reflects the linkages to the vegetable processing industry, and most output is sold to regional processors for eventual export throughout the country. The farms use some mechanization, and the family supplies almost all labor. Only one-third of the available labor (2.9 units) is utilized on the farm.

The specialized fruit system also shows the advantages of access to a relatively developed marketing chain. The system has an area of 13.2 ha, in only two parcels. The major crops are apples, olives, and vineyards. The farm is mechanized. Much of the labor needed is for harvesting and pruning and is hired. All output is sold to traders or through cooperatives.

The other distinctive system of the Litoral zone is rice. This farm is typical of the large irrigated perimeter in the Vale do Mondego. These systems are the consequence of substantial government investment in large scale irrigation works and land consolidation. The rice system has an area of 30 ha, making it one of the largest in the region. The farm is divided into only 7 plots, showing the marked effect of land consolidation programs on parcel size. About 60 percent of the land is used for irrigated rice; maize and wheat are the other crops. The system is highly mechanized, and some services, such as harvesting, are rented.

Table 3.2
Beira Litoral: main features of the farm systems

	Litoral				Intermediate			Planalto		Mountain	
	Rice	Medium Dairy	Traditional Olive/Wine	Vegetable	Specialized Fruit	Small Wine	Traditional	Fruits/Wine	Small Wine	Traditional	Medium Sheep
Crop land (ha)	29.7	7.10	8.55	1.2	13.2	3.2	4.44	11.18	4.15	2.22	12.81
Forest area (ha)	0	0	2.45	1.01	0	2.12	2.09	8.88	2.15	0	7.5
Rented area (%)	85	72	0	33	0	0	22	0	0	0	47
Irrigable area (%)	99	100	57	100	100	67	71	64	33	48	100
Irrigated area (%)	74	86	40	80	90	42	53	57	33	47	49
No of plots	7	11	10	5	2	15	7	5	5	8	5
Average distance (Km)	1.09	1.22	0.31	0.3	0.35	1.44	1.16	0.64	1.57	0.45	1.21
Prevalent activity											
Crops	Rice	Fodder crops	Wine	Horti-cultural	Fruits	Wine	Fodder crops	Fruits	Vineyard	Wine	Fodder crops
Livestock	Dairy cows	Dairy cows	Meat cows	Dairy cows		Pork	Dairy cows		Meat cows	Meat cows	Sheep & Goats
Forest	Pines		Mixed	Mixed		Pines	Pines	Mixed	Pines		Pines
Active family members:											
Off-farm employed FTE	0	0.2	0	0.2	0	0.3	0.1	0.4	0.6	0.4	0.2
On-farm employed: available FTE	2.3	2.70	2.20	3.10	1.02	1.60	3.10	2.40	2.00	1.60	3.77
utilized FTE	0.71	1.69	1.12	0.68	0.43	0.52	0.89	2.03	0.58	0.87	3.77

Source: Team survey

41

The systems that typify the rest of the Beira Litoral consist of a diverse set of orientations and differ widely in size - ranging from just over 2 ha to nearly 13 ha - and degree of commodity specialization. Many farms are similar to those found in the Minho. They tend to be less fragmented than Minho farms, but total size and production strategies (that emphasize diversification) often are similar. These zones are home to some of the most traditional (and poor) farms of the study. But other farms are more successful, and the specialized systems, oriented toward wine, fruit production, and sheep, make these zones distinct from other regions.. Demographic characteristics are similar: farmers are middle aged, little educated, and have families with much more labor available than is utilized by the farm system.

The Bairrada wine system is typical of a zone bordering on the Litoral. This farm is among the most fragmented farms of the region, having an area of 3.2 ha in 15 parcels. More than half the area is planted to vineyards, with the remainder given to maize, potatoes, and wheat. The farm has also forest land (2 ha) and produces young pigs for sale to the local market (leitao). The farm is little mechanized, and has 1.8 units of labor. Only a third of available labor is used.

The Planalto contains several systems. The relatively small farms are about 4 ha in size. The traditional farms have relatively ample supplies of irrigable land (71 percent) and produce a diversity of products. Most of the area is given to maize, forages, pasture, potatoes, and vineyards. The farm supports 3 dairy cows and a couple of calves. The farm has 2 ha of forest as well. The level of mechanization is low. The family has 3.1 units of available labor; less than one-third is utilized.

Another cohort of small farms in the Planalto zone shows much different characteristics. These farms have less irrigable land (33 percent) than the small diversified farm systems, and they tend to specialize in wine production. The small wine system uses 45 percent of the arable land for vineyards. The remaining area is used for pastures for beef production, maize, and apple orchards. Farmers tend to be much more educated than the diversified system farmers.

The final farm system of the Planalto zone has a production orientation similar to that of the small wine system but is larger, 11.2 ha. About 80 percent of the arable area is occupied by vineyards and fruit orchards. Most of the remainder is used for pasture for beef production. This farm system is notable also for its relatively large forest area (8.8 ha), used to grow a mixture of tree crops. Farmers from these systems have a medium level of education (secondary school) and are relatively young (average age is 46). Almost all family labor is utilized on the farm. Substantial labor is hired, mostly during the harvest season.

The systems of the mountain zone consist of small, traditional farms and larger sheep farms. The traditional system is only about 2 ha in size, growing maize, vineyards, potatoes, fruit trees and some horticultural crops for home consumption. A few beef animals are produced. Farm families have some access to off farm employment, especially in the form of emigration. Education levels are low and average ages are about 50. The Serra d'Estrela sheep system offers somewhat higher incomes. Average farm size is about 13 ha, with an

42

additional 7.5 ha of forest. More than 60 percent of the arable land is used to raise a herd of 68 sheep for milk production. This milk is converted to the well-known local cheese, queijo de serra. Potatoes and maize for silage are the other main crops. Farmers of this type tend to be relatively young (average age, 35) and have more education (secondary school) than the traditional farm types. This farm system is notable also for fully utilizing the family labor supply.

Oeste farming systems

A survey of 50 RICA farmers was used to construct a set of 8 representative farm systems for the Oeste (Table 3.3). Farms of this region are relatively large, ranging from 7 to 58 ha. Farms can be highly fragmented, half of the systems are comprised of at least 10 parcels, but average parcel size tends to be larger than those found in the more northern farm systems. Farms tend also to be relatively more mechanized.

The small and medium traditional systems produce a number of crops for market. The small farm system grows about equal areas of grapes (for wine and table grapes), orchards (pears, apples, and peaches), and forages for beef production. Farm operations are fully mechanized. The medium farm system has an identical cropping pattern but is nearly twice as large.

Other small farms have chosen different paths, usually more specialized in a particular commodity. The small dairy system has a herd of 10 dairy cows and 7 calves on an area of about 11 ha. More than 90 percent of the land is used for forage production, and a mobile milking technology is used. Another direction of specialization is represented by the vegetable farm system. Farm size is 7 ha, and about 60 percent of the area is used for an assortment of vegetables, including tomatoes, lettuce, green beans, and broccoli. These are sold in fresh markets and for freezing. Potatoes, vineyards, and fruit trees are the remaining crops. The final direction of specialization for small farms is represented by the specialized fruits system. About 80 percent of the area of this farm type is planted to apple and pear trees; vineyards and wheat also are grown. Many of the specialized farms utilize a large share of their family labor supplies; most need hired labor on a seasonal basis.

The remaining three farm systems are substantially larger size. The large dairy farm has an area of 58 ha and a herd of 102 animals, including 75 dairy cows. Milking systems are fully mechanized, and the farm uses full time salaried labor. The wine and fruit system is 35 ha. About 60 percent of the area is planted with apple and pear trees, and the remainder is given to vineyards (for wine and table grapes). Hired labor also is important in this system. The sheep system is 41 ha, almost all in natural pastures and rainfed forages. Herd size is 55 animals, used for meat and milk production.

Representativeness of the farming systems

The results of the 1989 Portuguese Farm Census were used to evaluate the representativeness of the 31 farming systems. Data in the Census permitted a correspondence to be established with the farm systems. The importance of representative farms was evaluated in terms of their shares in the number of farms and their share in cultivated area. The 11 systems for the Entre Douro e Minho represent 85 percent of the farms and 69 percent of the cultivated area of

43

Table 3.3
Oeste: main features of the farm systems

	Small dairy	Large dairy	Vegetable	Specialized Fruits	Fruits/ Wine	Small sheep	Small Traditional	Medium Traditional
Crop land (ha)	11.35	58	6.97	10.27	35.28	41.02	9.68	18.87
Forest area (ha)	0	0	0	0	4	0	0	0.5
Rented area (%)	69	10	43	17	0	14	7	7
Irrigable area (%)	60	37	100	100	59	44	11	66
Irrigated area (%)	25	37	83	76	9	0	11	16
No of plots	9	7	6	13	15	3	10	13
Average distance (Km)	1.23	0.47	1.77	1.64	2.57	1.13	0.81	1.64
Prevalent activity								
Crops	Fodder crops	Fodder crops	Horticultural	Fruits	Fruits	Fodder crops	Wine	Horticultural
Livestock	Dairy cows	Dairy cows				Sheep & Goats	Meat cows	
Forest					Eucalyptus			Eucalyptus
Active family members:								
Off-farm employed FTE	0.4	0.6	0.3	0.1	0.6	0.7	0.4	0.1
On-farm employed:available FTE	1.70	1.35	1.80	2.30	4.09	1.55	2.60	2.00
utilized FTE	0.60	0.69	1.15	2.10	4.09	1.06	1.34	0.39

Source: Team survey

44

the region; the 11 systems for the Beira Litoral represent 61 percent of the farms and 56 percent of the area; and the 9 systems for the Oeste represent 81 percent of the farms and 65 percent of the area. The weights of each representative system in the total farm population are shown in Table 3.4.

The Minho is the most important region, accounting for nearly half of the cultivated area and the number of farms. The Beira Litoral accounts for about one third of the totals, and Oeste region makes up the remainder. A few representative systems are of special importance. The diversified systems of the Mountain zone in Entre Douro e Minho, the Planalto of Beira Litoral, and Oeste together account for more than 60 percent of farm numbers and 50 percent of cultivated area. Also important is the beef system of the Mountain zone in the Minho. This system, limited by lack of irrigation water and geographical conditions, accounts for a little more than 10 percent of farm numbers and cultivated area. None of the other systems accounts for more than 2 percent of the regional totals, showing the distinct lack of specialization in market orientation of small farm agriculture.

Baseline economic results

The calculations of present and potential future performance were based on budgets of costs and returns of alternative commodities and technologies. The budgets were based on secondary information, adjusted for information obtained from field surveys. The 'standard' budgets represent costs and returns on an ideally shaped parcel of one ha in size. These estimates are modified within the farm model as necessary to recognize the impacts of less optimal parcel structures. The structural characteristics of the farm - mainly the types of roads and quality of access to the parcels - determine the inputs and costs involved in reaching each of the farm's parcels. Farm structure also affects input requirements relative to the standard one hectare budget. The most important information in this category is the shape and total area of the parcel.

The principal crops of the Entre Douro e Minho region are maize, potatoes, silage, forages, permanent pastures, vineyards, orchards, and horticultural crops. The crops are produced under varying degrees of mechanization and with different levels of intermediate inputs. In total, 80 budgets were developed to represent the alternative modes of producing the commodities. The most important animal product is milk, and six technologies are represented. These differ in terms of breed, input levels, and milking technology. Seven technologies are represented in the production of beef. Single budgets are used to represent costs and returns to sheep and goat production. The latter system is found only in the mountain zone and farms show little variation in production technology.

Principal crops of the Beira Litoral region are maize, potatoes, horticultural crops (sometimes grown in greenhouses), industrial horticultural crops, rice, olives, tobacco, rainfed cereals, silage, forages, and permanent pastures. Ninety-nine budgets were used to represent this diverse group of crops and technologies. The principal animal production activities are milk (6 budgets),

Table 3.4
Representativeness of the Northern and Central Portugal farming systems

Entre Douro e Minho	N⁰ Farms	SAU(ha)	(%) N⁰	(%) SAU
Litoral - Large Dairy	714	9263	0.34	2.17
Vegetable	1758	2145	0.85	0.50
Medium Dairy	627	4063	0.30	0.95
Small Dairy	2298	8663	1.11	2.03
Intermédiate-Medium Dairy	561	4853	0.27	1.14
Medium Wine	214	2116	0.10	0.50
Small Dairy	2989	10720	1.44	2.52
Small Wine	3080	11581	1.48	2.72
Mountain- Small Sheep	451	1173	0.22	0.28
Traditional	60151	85204	28.98	19.99
Traditional Beef	21921	54773	10.56	12.85
Beira Litoral				
Litoral- Rice	93	2148	0.04	0.50
Medium Dairy	369	1970	0.18	0.46
Traditional Olive/Wine	352	1756	0.17	0.41
Small Vegetable	259	277	0.12	0.06
Intermediate- Specialized Fruit	50	544	0.02	0.13
Intermediate- Small Wine	2500	6950	1.20	1.63
Traditional	56534	89497	27.24	21.00
Planalto- Fruit/Wine	82	463	0.04	0.11
Small Wine	1863	7024	0.90	1.65
Mountain- Medium Sheep	248	2262	0.12	0.53
Mountain- Traditional	13141	17740	6.33	4.16
Oeste				
Large Dairy	91	3983	0.04	0.93
Vegetable	1736	11805	0.84	2.77
Specialized Fruit	1337	9252	0.64	2.17
Medium Traditional	281	2492	0.14	0.58
Small Dairy	1161	5828	0.56	1.37
Small Sheep	1161	10032	0.56	2.35
Fruits/Wine	734	11069	0.35	2.60
Small Traditional	30819	46537	14.85	10.92
Totals:				
EDM	94764	194554	45.65	45.65
BL	75491	130631	36.37	30.65
Oeste	37320	100998	17.98	23.70
TOTALS	207575	426183	100	100

Sources: Team estimates; Agricultural Census

sheep for milk or meat (12 budgets), and pork for the production of suckling pigs (2 budgets).

In the Oeste region, the principal crops are horticultural products, grown in the fields or in greenhouses. Thirty budgets were used to describe the rich diversity of systems in this product class. Other specialty crops include orchards (10 budgets), flowers in greenhouses (2 budgets), and vineyards for table wine (6 budgets). Cereal crops are principally rainfed (7 budgets), as are silage (4 budgets), and pastures (5 budgets). Among animal production systems, the principal products are milk (6 budgets), and sheep for meat (4 budgets).

The main outputs of the farm model are costs, returns, and farm profits. The costs are divided among categories of inputs - intermediate inputs, capital, and labor. The total returns to the farm are divided among crops, animal products, and secondary by-products. The net farm returns are represented in two ways. The long-run perspective estimates the net returns to family labor by considering all other inputs at their opportunity costs. The short-run perspective considers all owned inputs as sunk costs. The model also generates a calendar of total labor use, which is useful in linking the farm model results to different scenarios about family demographic structure and off farm employment opportunities.

Baseline results were based on the price and subsidy system of 1992 (Table 3.5). This baseline represents well the set of price incentives for the first half of the 1990s. The systems show much variation in profitability. In the short-run, all systems except the small traditional farm of Oeste have at least positive net returns to family labor. But in the long-run perspective, many of the systems have negative profits. The relatively large or specialized systems fare the best. In the Minho, the highest returns are earned by the largest of the dairy systems, the horticulture system, and the specialized wine system. In the other zones, relatively large dairy systems and specialized systems - rice, fruit or horticulture - offer returns that often are well above off-farm earnings. These profitable systems tend to have relatively large intermediate input, capital and land costs as well. Entry into these systems is not easy for many small farmers. In contrast, the traditional systems in each of the zones offer returns that are low, frequently much below, off-farm wage rates. These systems are much more common in the study area than the more specialized and more profitable systems. Even in the short-run, many farmers would do better financially if they could abandon farming and find off-farm employment.

The results of Table 3.5 are organized by regions - Entre Douro e Minho (EDM), Beira Litoral (BL), and Oeste (O) - and aggregated in Table 3.6. In total, 19 of the 31 systems were not competitive in the baseline. Family labor inputs were not rewarded with returns comparable to those paid by alternative off farm employment. This condition was worst in the EDM (8 of 11). The best relative situation was in Oeste (4 of the 9 systems were competitive). The poor economic performance is even more evident at the aggregate level. Only 3.4 percent of farms and only 10.5 percent of arable land offer competitive rates of return to labor. Most of the non-competitive farms (44.2 percent) and area (96.6 percent) are located in the EDM. About half of the competitive land area is located in the Oeste.

Table 3.5
Economic results, farm systems, baseline year (1992)

System	Revenues	Intermediate inputs	Capital	Land	Hired Labor	Total returns/year	Returns to labor/day	
							Long-run	Short-run
		contos ('000 Escudos)						
Entre Douro e Minho								
Litoral								
Small Dairy	2964	957	462	490	869	186	0.46	2.11
Medium Dairy	6006	2900	1176	703	1015	212	0.48	2.02
Large Dairy	18296	7358	2816	1643	1546	4933	7.12	7.35
Vegetable	4188	519	167	470	541	2491	10.38	11.30
Intermediate								
Small Dairy	3139	1411	623	516	946	-357	-0.83	0.86
Medium Dairy	8184	3599	1571	905	901	1208	2.98	3.06
Small vineyard	2375	755	484	557	720	-141	-0.43	1.01
Medium wine	4824	996	740	967	480	1640	11.71	10.28
Mountain								
Traditional	738	194	95	159	359	-69	-0.36	1.14
Sheep and Goats	744	62	158	76	333	115	0.66	2.20
Traditional Beef	1659	528	439	521	1232	-1061	-1.93	0.09
Beira Litoral								
Litoral								
Rice	8123	3792	1635	1002	519	1176	6.63	7.16
Medium Dairy	6314	3098	1151	352	1159	553	1.31	3.16
Traditional Olive/Wine	2451	722	406	271	765	287	1.03	2.87
Vegetable	1858	379	86	176	387	829	4.88	6.15
Intermediate								
Specialized fruit	8931	1526	2646	1154	752	2852	26.53	4.76
Small wine	743	287	236	99	421	-299	-2.30	0.48
Traditional	1024	449	191	147	482	-244	-1.10	0.74
Planalto								
Fruits/Wine	6701	2204	1317	603	1644	933	1.84	3.02
Small wine	1680	650	249	137	421	223	1.54	2.43
Mountain								
Traditional	1795	1092	259	88	421	-65	-0.30	1.21
Medium Sheep	4903	1150	579	482	1875	817	0.87	2.05
Oeste								
Small Dairy	3234	1342	427	126	613	726	4.84	7.43
Large Dairy	36902	13214	6662	1255	3101	12670	73.45	29.69
Vegetable	4326	1164	323	358	1376	1105	3.84	6.61
Specialized fruit	8169	2125	1309	602	2533	1600	3.05	5.69
Fruits/Wine	13554	4932	2431	1844	5984	-1637	-1.60	0.44
Small Sheep	2032	631	294	87	867	153	0.58	2.00
Small Traditional	2594	1125	664	343	1470	-1008	-3.01	-0.01
Medium Traditional	726	257	149	55	331	-67	-0.69	2.04

Source: Team estimates

48

Table 3.6 shows also the irrelevance of direct support measures to competitiveness of small farm agriculture. Most of the competitive systems receive very little in subsidies. In terms of product orientation, the most profitable systems are those oriented toward irrigated crops (4 in 12), wine (2), and dairy production (5). Most of the profitable systems are located in the litoral zones of each region. Their production patterns emphasize commodities that are largely outside the CAP. Among the CAP commodities, such as maize, subsidies are too small to increase returns a substantial amount.

Most of the non-competitive systems (16 of 19) are viable in the short run. If fixed costs are considered sunk and all net farm returns are attributed to family labor, the rate of return is higher than the off farm wage rate. But in terms of farm numbers and area cultivated, viability is small. Less than one-third of the non-competitive farms and only 40 percent of the non-competitive area remain viable. For the rest of the non-competitive systems, farm families would do better financially if they could find off farm employment. The economic situation is healthier for the Oeste region, where all the non-competitive systems are viable.

This poor economic performance is related in part to the agro-technological and socio-structural limitations characteristic of this type of small farm agriculture. The other part of the explanation is the 50 percent decline in agricultural prices in Portugal between 1985 and 1992. This decline (in real terms) reflects the effects of Portugal's harmonization with EC and CAP policies and the substantial appreciation of the escudo.

Future competitiveness of farming systems

Future competitiveness of the Portuguese farming systems is estimated by modification of the baseline model and results. Output, input, and domestic factor prices and income supports are projected to the post-MacSharry reform period to generate a projected baseline result for each of the farm systems. This result reflects the impact of changes in incentives, without allowing for any adjustment by farmers. The effects of the projected prices on farm incentives are summarized in Table 3.7. This table contains summary results for the northern and central Portuguese region and separate results for the three regions of Entre Douro e Minho, Beira Litoral, and Oeste.

The CAP reform will reduce by one (from 12 to 11) the number of competitive systems. Only one of the systems depends on direct supports to be competitive. However, the importance of competitive systems in the region will increase. The share of competitive farms increases from 3.4 percent to 18.4 percent in terms of total numbers and from 10.5 percent to 21.7 percent in terms of cultivated area. The gains are found largely in the Oeste region. CAP reform has a negative impact on the EDM and BL systems. The improvement in Oeste is the result of expected increases in horticulture and fruit prices, a consequence of the assumed termination of overvaluation of the escudo. The diversified permanent crop systems thus increase in profitability under CAP reform and full integration with the EC. Future expansion of these systems requires the expansion of attractive marketing systems as well as growth in

Table 3.6
Competitiveness of Northern and Central Portugal farming systems, 1992

Type of Systems	No of systems				No of farms (percent)				Arable land (percent)			
	EDM	BL	O	Total	EDM	BL	O	Total	EDM	BL	O	Total
Competitive w/out direct support	3	5	4	12	1.5	0.4	1.5	3.4	3.8	1.6	5.1	10.5
Competitive with direct support	0	0	0	0	0.0	0.0	0.0	0.0	0.0	0.0	0.0	0.0
Non-competitive but viable in the short run	6	5	5	16	4.7	8.6	16.5	29.8	9.0	8.1	18.6	35.7
Noncompetitive and non-viable	2	1	0	3	39.5	27.3	0.0	66.8	32.8	21.0	0.0	53.8
TOTALS	11	11	9	31	45.7	36.3	18.0	100.0	45.6	30.7	23.7	100.0

Source: Team estimates

Table 3.7
Northern and Central Portugal and projected competitiveness, Post-MacSharry

Northern and Central Portugal	Baseline prices			Projected prices		
	No of systems	No of farms	Arable land	No of systems	No of farms	Arable land
		(percent)	(percent)		(percent)	(percent)
Competitive w/out direct support	12	3.4	10.5	10	17.8	19.3
Competitive with direct support	0	0.0	0.0	1	0.6	2.4
Non-competitive but viable in the short run	16	29.8	35.7	15	12.2	20.4
Noncompetitive and non-viable	3	66.8	53.8	5	69.4	58.0
TOTAL	31	100	100	31	100	100
Entre Douro e Minho						
Competitive w/out direct support	3	3.2	8.4	2	2.6	5.9
Competitive with direct support	0	0.0	0.0	0	0.0	0.0
Non-competitive but viable in the short run	6	10.2	19.7	6	7.6	16.7
Noncompetitive and non-viable	2	86.6	71.9	3	89.8	77.5
TOTAL	11	100.0	100.0	11	100.0	100.0
Beira Litoral						
Competitive w/out direct support	5	1.5	5.1	3	0.9	2.0
Competitive with direct support	0	0.0	0.0	0	0.0	0.0
Non-competitive but viable in the short run	5	23.6	26.4	6	20.9	24.2
Noncompetitive and non-viable	1	74.9	68.5	2	78.2	73.8
TOTAL	11	100.0	100.0	11	100.0	100.0
Oeste						
Competitive w/out direct support	4	8.0	21.4	5	90.6	67.5
Competitive with direct support	0	0.0	0.0	1	3.1	9.9
Non-competitive but viable in the short run	5	92.0	78.6	3	6.3	22.6
Noncompetitive and non-viable	0	0.0	0.0	0	0.0	0.0
TOTAL	9	100.0	100.0	9	100.0	100.0

Source: Team estimates

51

production. The CAP reform has little impact on subsidies and income transfers to the farming systems, and the aggregate impact on Northern and Central agriculture is small. Most commodities are not directly affected by the expected changes in CAP policies.

The research team next identified possible changes in crop mix or technologies for each of the farm systems. These changes reflected feasible changes in private and public investment. Introduction of these changes into the farm model simulates the potential economic incentives after CAP reform. The feasibility of these changes at the macroeconomic level is assessed by comparing the funds available from the 1994-99 Community Structural Framework with the potential costs of public and private investment implied by the farm system simulations. Such a comparison shows the feasibility of a comprehensive dissemination of the simulated techniques. Further changes were identified based on the implementation of the CAP reforms. The most important reforms were those concerned with the conversion to forest and the expansion of environmentally friendly crop systems.

In the EDM litoral zone the changes were based on the further specialization of the existing dairy and horticultural systems (Figure 3.1). The dairy systems were hypothesized to uproot low quality vineyards, increase irrigated forage and maize area, and thus expand the dairy herd. Private and public investments in irrigation, electrification, and feeder roads were introduced to each of the farms where relevant and feasible. The main changes to the horticultural system involved increase of water available for irrigation and increases in the irrigated area. Electrification and feeder road improvement were relevant also for these systems, because they affected technology choices, such as electrical pumps and the use of mechanical harvesters for forage and maize.

Changes in the EDM intermediate zone were similar to those for the Litoral zone dairy farms. For the wine systems, the changes simulated improvements of vineyards by changing varieties (in favor of Loureiro), types of wine (white in favor of red vinho verde), and the structure of the vine support systems (the 'cordao' system was assumed to replace the traditional ramada system). Secondary crops were affected by the restructuring of vineyards, allowing changes in technologies. Public investments in feeder roads were the most important investment in this zone.

Changes in the EDM mountain zone emphasized the new CAP provisions to introduce forest and environmentally friendly crop systems. Some changes in crops and technologies were possible because of simulated improvements in traditional irrigation systems and regional feeder roads. But options for change were fewer in this zone, reflecting its disadvantaged status.

In Beira Litoral, the simulations emphasized changes similar to those considered for the EDM (Figure 3.2). In the Litoral zone, each farming system was assumed to increase the degree of specialization in its principal commodity. Simultaneously, the farms were assumed to introduce improved technologies. Public investments in irrigation, electrification, and feeder road improvement were considered for all parcels and introduced where technically feasible and economically attractive. Uprooting of low quality vineyards was important in allowing many of the farm system to expand their most profitable crops (often vegetables and fruits).

Farming systems	Crop mix or technological changes	Vineyards		Private and Public investments	Forestry and agro-environmental conversion
		Improvement	Uprooting		
Litoral					
Small dairy	X		X	I/FR/E	
Medium dairy	X		X	I/FR/E	
Large dairy	X		X	I/FR/E	
Horticulture	X			I/FR	
Intermediate					
Small dairy	X		X	I/FR	
Medium dairy	X		X	FR	
Small wine	X	X		FR	
Medium wine	X	X		FR/E	
Mountain					
Diversified	X			I/FR	F/A
Sheep and Goat				I/FR	F/A
Small beef	X		X	I/FR/E	F/A

I - irrigation investments; FR - feeder roads; E - electrification; F - forestry conversion; A - agro-environmental conversion

Figure 3.1 Modifications applied to Entre Douro e Minho farming systems

Farming systems	Crop mix and/or technological changes	Vineyards		Private and Public investments	Forestry and agro-environmental conversion
		Improvement	Uprooting		
Litoral					
Medium dairy	X			I/FR/E	
Horticulture	X		X	I/FR/E	
Rice	X				
Wine and Olive	X				
Fruit - growing	X		X	I/FR/E	
Intermediate					
Small wine	X	X		I	
Planalto					
Diversified	X			I/FR/E	F/A
Small wine	X	X		FR	
Wine and Fruit	X			I/FR/E	
Mountain					
Diversified	X		X		F/A
Sheep	X			FR	

I - irrigation investments; FR - feeder roads; E - electrification; F - forestry conversion; A - agro-environmental conversion

Figure 3.2 Modifications applied to Beira Litoral farming systems

54

In the interior zones of Beira Litoral (Bairrada, Planalto, and Serra), simulations varied by type of farm. Changes in the diversified farm systems emphasized the introduction of forestry and environmentally friendly crop systems. Simulations of the wine systems assumed improvements in vine quality and support systems; analogous changes were introduced to the fruit orchard systems. Sheep systems were changed by improving the productivity of natural pastures and the quality of the herd. This change allowed subsequent improvement in the quality of milk produced for cheese, a product that is already well known in the Portuguese market. Potential public investments were considered as well.

In the Oeste region, the simulations emphasize private investments in irrigation and electrification. Such changes are important to allow the farm systems to increase their specialization and modernize (Figure 3.3). These changes were important especially for the fruit and horticultural systems. Improvement of irrigated forage and maize production was important for the Oeste dairy systems and allowed a quantitative and qualitative change in the herd. Some variety improvements were introduced into the fruit crop systems. As in the other regions, low quality vineyards were uprooted and forestry area was expanded, taking advantage of the new direct subsidy programs.

Returns improve considerably as a result of the simulated changes (Table 3.8). The number of competitive systems increases from 11 to 25. The share of competitive farm systems increases from 18 to 52 percent and the share of cultivated area increases from 22 to 59 percent. Adjustments by the farm sector and further investments in the agricultural sector make a substantial improvement in the rates of return to small farm agriculture. The mountain areas remain in difficult straits. But for the rest of the region, competitiveness appears attainable.

In the EDM, nine of the 11 systems show competitiveness, but these represent only 13 percent of the farms and 28 percent of the cultivated area in the zones of the EDM. The interior zones remain largely unaffected by change in public or private investment. In Beira Litoral, a majority of farms and most of the agricultural area gain competitiveness as a result of the simulated changes. This shift results especially from improvements in the fruit, wine, and vegetable systems and the benefits for conversion to forestry and the environmentally friendly crop systems. The number of competitive systems increases relative to the post-MacSharry baseline from 3 to 9. The results for the Oeste also show improvements in competitiveness. However, the improvements are not so substantial as in the other zones, highlighting the relative attractiveness of the Oeste systems in the baseline situation. Change in this region is less critical than in the other regions. The importance of fruit and horticultural crops means that the traditional CAP programs have little relevance for many of these systems; they are affected most significantly by the assumed reforms in macroeconomic policies and revision in the value of the escudo.

Categorization of systems by potential competitiveness shows that change is critical to small farm agriculture (Table 3.9). About one-third of the systems (11 of 31) will be able to compete without further change, but these systems represent only 19 percent of the farms and 23 percent of the cultivated area; these farms are concentrated in the Oeste region. But 13 of the systems are

| Farming systems | Crop mix and/or technological changes | Vineyards | | Private and Public investments | Forestry and agro-environmental conversion |
		Improvement	Uprooting		
Small permanent crops	X			I/E	F
Medium permanent crops	X				F
Small dairy	X			I/E	
Large dairy	X			I/E	
Horticulture	X		X	E	
Fruit - growing	X		X		
Wine and Fruit	X	X		I/E	
Sheep	X		X		

I - irrigation investments; FR - feeder roads; E - electrification; F - forestry conversion; A - agro-environmental conversion

Figure 3.3   Modifications applied to Oeste farming systems

56

Table 3.8
Northern and Central farming systems, projected competitiveness, with technical and crop charges

Northern and Central Portugal	No of systems	Projected prices without crop mix and/or technological changes (percent)		Projected prices with crop mix or technological changes (percent)		
		No of farms	Arable land	No of systems	No of farms	Arable land
Competitive without direct support	10	17.8	19.3	21	22.4	33.2
Competitive with direct support	1	0.6	2.4	4	30.1	25.4
Non-competitive but viable in the short run	15	12.2	20.4	5	18.6	21.4
Noncompetitive and non-viable	5	69.4	58.0	1	29.0	20.0
TOTAL	31	100.0	100.0	31	100.0	100.0
Entre Douro e Minho						
Competitive without direct support	2	2.6	5.9	7	9.8	21.9
Competitive with direct support	0	0.0	0.0	2	3.6	6.1
Non-competitive but viable in the short run	6	7.6	16.7	1	23.1	28.2
Noncompetitive and non-viable	3	89.8	77.5	1	63.5	43.8
TOTAL	11	100.0	100.0	11	100.0	100.0
Beira Litoral						
Competitive without direct support	3	0.0	0.0	7	1.9	7.2
Competitive with direct support	0	0.9	2.0	2	78.2	73.8
Non-competitive but viable in the short run	6	20.9	24.2	2	19.9	19.0
Noncompetitive and non-viable	2	78.2	73.8	0	0.0	0.0
TOTAL	11	100.0	100.0	11	100.0	100.0
Oeste						
Competitive without direct support	5	90.6	67.5	7	95.7	88.4
Competitive with direct support	1	3.1	9.9	0	0.0	0.0
Non-competitive but viable in the short run	3	6.3	22.6	2	4.3	11.6
Noncompetitive and non-viable	0	0.0	0.0	0	0.0	0.0
TOTAL	9	100.0	100.0	9	100.0	100.0

Source: Team estimates

Table 3.9
Classification of Northern and Central Portugal farming systems according to competitiveness

Type of Systems	EDM			BL			Oeste			Total		
	No of systems	No of farms	Arable land	No of systems	No of farms	Arable land	No of systems	No of farms	Arable land	No of systems	No of farms	Arable land
		(percent)			(percent)			(percent)			(percent)	
Competitive	2	1.4	4.2	3	0.3	0.6	6	16.8	18.3	11.0	18.5	23.1
Potentially competitive	7	15.0	21.2	5	28.7	23.7	1	0.4	2.6	13.0	44.	47.5
Non-competitive	2	29.2	20.3	3	7.4	6.3	2	0.8	2.8	7.0	37.4	29.4
TOTAL	11	45.6	45.7	11	36.4	30.6	9	18.0	23.7	31.0	100	100

Source: Team estimates

58

potentially competitive with the simulated changes, and these systems account for 44 percent of the farms and 48 percent of cultivated area. These changes are especially important in the Beira Litoral region. More than 35 percent of the farms and 30 percent of the area remains non-competitive, even with the changes. These farms are especially important in the EDM and most prominent in the Intermediate and Mountain zones. For these farms, structural change probably means exit from the agricultural sector.

Implications for structural change

The effect of structural adjustments on rural areas in Northern and Central Portugal and the kinds of policies that are needed to ease the process of structural adjustment are the principal concerns of policy. Changes in price and subsidy policies and subsequent adjustments in crop mix and technologies will have implications for structural change. These structural adjustments are associated with three different circumstances involving farming systems. First, non-competitive systems will be expected eventually to release their farm population to alternative off farm employment. The competitive systems, if they are located in areas with inflexible labor and land markets, will find also that on farm employment can not be sustained. They will tend to leave agriculture, not because the rate of return to their resources is too small, but because the total remuneration is not comparable to what can be earned off the farm. They would desire to increase their farm size or find off farm employment for at least some of the family labor force. But in areas where this is not possible, emigration becomes the only solution. The third group of farms involved in structural change will include potentially competitive systems that are able to increase in size. These opportunities should arise in the areas with flexible factor markets; even in areas with factor markets that are traditionally inflexible, outmigration from agriculture would make some land resources available to those who remain in the sector.

In assessing the autonomy of the farming systems (Table 3.10), it appears that only 51 percent of the farms and 59 percent of the area are autonomous or potentially autonomous. Almost half of the farm systems will be unable to generate an income of at least one FTE. Only part of the non-autonomous farms (37 percent of the total population) offer non-competitive returns, meaning that only about 11 percent of the farms can attain autonomy through structural adjustment. But for most non-autonomous farms, outmigration from agriculture seems likely to be an important alternative in the future.

In terms of absorption of available family labor, only 7 of the 31 systems, representing about 37 percent of the number of farms, will be unable to absorb the available family labor supply (Table 3.10). Among the remaining systems, most will require changes in crop mix and technologies to absorb family labor; such changes are necessary on 61 percent of the farms and 65 percent of the cultivated area. These changes are formidable; in addition, many of these farms require increases in farm size.

Only 5 of the systems (1 percent of farms and 5 percent of area) will be able to avoid changes in structure, technology, or crop mix (Table 3.11). About 60

59

Table 3.10
Classification of Northern and Central Portugal farming systems according to autonomy and absorption of family labor surplus

	No of systems				No of farms (percent)				Arable land (percent)			
	EDM	BL	O	Total	EDM	BL	O	Total	EDM	BL	O	Total
Autonomy (≥1 FTE)												
Autonomous	5	6	7	18	2.8	0.7	3	6.5	6.9	1.7	12.2	20.8
Potentially autonomous	3	2	1	6	3.0	27.3	15	42.2	5.7	21.5	10.9	38.1
Non-Autonomous	3	3	1	7	39.8	8.4	0	48.3	33.1	7.4	0.6	41.1
TOTAL	11	11	9	31	45.6	36.4	18	18.0	45.7	30.6	23.7	100
Family labor supply												
With capacity of absorption	2	2	2	6	1.4	0.2	0.0	1.6	4.2	0.6	0.9	5.7
With potential capacity of absorption	7	6	5	18	15.0	28.8	17.2	61.0	21.2	23.7	20.0	64.9
Without capacity of absorption	2	3	2	7	29.2	7.4	0.8	37.4	20.3	6.3	2.8	29.4
TOTAL	11	11	9	31	45.6	36.4	18.0	100	45.7	30.6	23.7	100

Source: Team estimates

Table 3.11
Classification of Northern and Central Portugal farming systems by long run viability and future structural impact

Type of Systems	No of systems				No of farms (percent)				Arable land (percent)			
	EDM	BL	O	Total	EDM	BL	O	Total	EDM	BL	O	Total
Viable and Competitive	2	1	2	5	1.4	0.0	0.0	1.4	4.2	0.1	0.9	5.2
Viable but Potentially Competitive		1		1	-	0.2	-	0.2	-	0.5	-	0.5
Potentially Viable but Competitive		2	4	6	-	0.3	16.8	17.1	-	0.5	17.4	17.9
Potentially Viable and Potentially Competitive	7	4	1	12	15.0	28.5	0.4	43.9	21.2	23.2	2.6	47.0
Non-Competitive	2	3	2	7	29.2	7.4	0.8	37.4	20.3	6.3	2.8	29.4
TOTALS	11	11	9	31	45.6	36.4	18.0	100	45.7	30.6	23.7	100
With Neutral Structural Impact	-	-	-	0	-	-	-	0.0	-	-	-	0.0
With Necessary Structural Impact	2	3	2	7	29.2	7.4	0.8	37.4	20.3	6.3	2.8	29.4
With a Potential Structural Impact	9	8	7	24	16.4	29.0	17.2	62.6	25.4	24.3	20.9	70.6
TOTALS	11	11	9	31	45.6	36.4	18.0	100	45.7	30.6	23.7	100

Source: Team estimates

61

percent of the farms and 66 percent of the cultivated area will require significant adjustment to accommodate the new CAP policies and remain in agriculture. The rest of the farms will have ample incentives to leave the sector. About 17 percent of farms and cultivated area depend exclusively on increases in farm size or increased off farm employment to maintain viability. About 44 percent of the farms will need to adjust simultaneously their crop mix and their farm size to remain viable. Few farms can remain viable only with changes in crop mix and technologies (Table 3.11). Nonviable systems represent 37 percent of farms and 29 percent of the area; these farms will have an effective structural impact because they will supply land to other farmers, and labor to the off farm labor market. The remaining farms will have an interest in the factor markets also, because their available labor supply exceeds the demands of the simulated farm systems.

Structural change thus could affect almost all farms in Northern and Central Portugal. Regions differ only in terms of the relative importance of the types of adjustment needed (Table 3.12). Increases in farm size or off farm employment are the most important ways to sustain long run viability in the Oeste region; changes in crop mix and technologies are the main changes in Beira Litoral; and farmers in the Entre Douro e Minho depend mainly on off farm employment or other sources of income (such as retirement pensions or direct income transfers).

Conclusion

Portugal still has considerable distance to go in the process of structural change. Outmigration has been substantial in recent decades and appears likely to continue. It will be a particularly strong change without further change. Without modernization of most of the systems and substantial public investments in agricultural infrastructure, about four-fifths of the farm area and an even greater proportion of farms will have ample incentive to leave agriculture. But quite different outcomes are possible. About three-fourths of the farms and two-thirds of the cultivated area have the potential to be competitive and remain in agriculture. Many of them would be part-time farms, pointing to the importance of non-agricultural development policies that will affect firm location and worker access. These are important complements to agricultural policies for investment and provision of public goods. Without public policies in these areas, accelerated outmigration from the sector seems a certainty.

Table 3.12
Importance of different adjustments, by region

Type of Systems	EDM		BL		Oeste	
	No of farms	Arable land	No of farms	Arable land	No of farms	Arable land
	(percent)					
Crop mix and/or technological change	-	-	0.6	1.6	-	-
Farm size and/or off farm employment increases	-	-	0.9	1.6	93.3	76.3
Both types of adjustments	33.9	51.0	78.4	76.2	2.2	11.4
Off farm employment or other income sources	66.1	49.0	20.1	20.6	4.5	12.3
TOTAL	100.0	100.0	100.0	100.0	100.0	100.0

Source: Team estimates

63

4 Small farms in Southern Italy

Carlo Cafiero, Antonio Cioffi, Paolo Cupo,
Eugenio Pomarici and Fabrizio Sallusti

Small farms in southern Italy represent an extraordinarily diverse group of commodities, production strategies, and agro-environmental conditions. At one extreme are capital-intensive businesses producing high-valued crops (such as flowers) with technically sophisticated methods in urban areas (particularly Naples). These operations offer returns as high as any industries in the economy. At the other extreme are the operations more typical of Mezzogiorno agriculture - relatively uneducated farmers in isolated areas, facing limited opportunities in crop mix and technology choice. Their incomes are as low as any in the economy.

This characterization overlooks the substantial change that small farm agriculture has experienced in recent decades. Farms are much larger and more consolidated than they once were. All farms are mechanized, and almost all are well-integrated into marketing systems and European agricultural policy incentives. Implementation of explicit structural adjustment programs has been limited, but the exact reasons for such limited implementation are not clear. They would seem not due to the behavior or attitudes of farmers; the rapid mechanization of the agricultural sector during the 1980s in response to very substantial capital subsidy programs gives ample indication of the capacity of the sector to respond to economic incentive. Southern agriculture has not been unaffected by the enormous economic change that has taken place in Italy during the last 50 years.

The research team from the Centro di Specializzazione e Ricerche Economico Agrarie per il Mezzogiorno (CSREAM) assessed prospects for further change in the small farm sector of southern Italy. Structural adjustment processes are accelerated when prices change, as will happen when the CAP reform and GATT agreements take full effect. The gradual substitution of market price support measures with EC prices close to world market levels, direct subsidies to producers, and supply management measures will put pressure both on farmers and on the government institutions charged with supporting

65

agriculture. Implementation of price policies, relatively straightforward for local administrations, will not be so important as attempts to disseminate new technologies, new crops, and new marketing arrangements. These latter types of change require more initiative from local organizations than did past European policy.

Farms most influenced by the price and subsidy changes will be those that emphasize grains, dairy, beef, sugar beets, processed tomatoes, and tobacco. Areas producing these commodities received particular attention in this study: Potenza province, because of the importance of beef, durum wheat, and dairy products; Avellino province, where the most important products are durum wheat and tobacco; Campobasso province, because of durum wheat and sugar beets; and Foggia province, where durum wheat, processed tomatoes, and sugar beets are important crops. Within each of these four provinces, limited areas were chosen to ensure emphasis on the most sensitive commodities (Map 4.1). The study areas were Alta Val d'Agri (in Potenza), Ufita and Alta Irpinia (in Avellino), and Basso Molise and Alta Capitanata (in Campobasso and Foggia provinces). Selection of these areas is not attempt to capture the huge diversity of southern agriculture; instead, they are the areas most likely to be affected by the MacSharry reforms and thus under the greatest pressure to adjust.

Description of the selected zones

Alta Val d'Agri belongs entirely to Potenza province and includes 11 communi, covering about 640 sq kms. The zone has one of the lowest population densities in the Mezzogiorno. The population is relatively old, and literacy rates are low. Agriculture accounts for 20 percent of total employment, although this share is declining. Part-time farming is relatively prominent, especially among younger farmers. After agriculture, construction is the largest source of employment; this sector accounts for almost all industrial activity in the zone.

Average farm size in Val d'Agri is 10.8 ha (6.6 ha of cropland), but this average conceals substantial inequality. Sixteen percent of the farms account for 64 percent of total area. Only a small part of agricultural land (about 6 percent) is irrigated. An equally small share is planted in permanent crops. Around 60 percent of agricultural land is pasture, and the remainder is devoted to annual crops. Livestock is by far the most important agricultural activity. Sheep and goats are dominant, and their population grew 72 percent between 1982 and 1990. Average herd size is 40 head. Dairy and beef have diminished in importance in recent years.

The Ufita-Alta Irpinia zone, in Avellino province, has demographic characteristics similar to those of Val d'Agri. This zone is larger than Val d'Agri, including 27 communi covering 1125 sq kms. Population density is relatively sparse. The low literacy rate has increased in recent years. Agriculture accounts for 23 percent of employment, but is declining. Part time farming is not very common, involving about a fourth of farm households. Part time operations often are combined with jobs in building and construction. The farm population is relatively aged.

Map 4.1   Study areas in Southern Italy

Farm structure also has characteristics similar to Val d'Agri. Farms are small, averaging 4.5 ha. Land is unequally distributed, and 10 percent of the farms operate half of the arable area. Irrigation is unimportant, accounting only for 2 percent of cropped area. The area differs from Val d'Agri in cropping patterns. In Avellino, annual crops dominate, durum wheat and tobacco being of particular importance. Cereals account for two-thirds of the cropped area. Only 12 percent of the area is in pastures. Sheep and goats are the most common herds, but the importance of livestock is declining rapidly. Herd size is smaller than in the other zones.

A very different agriculture is represented by the Basso Molise-Alta Capitanata zone. This region includes 18 communi (11 in Foggia province and the rest in Campobasso province), covering 2600 sq kms. This zone is the only one studied with increasing population trends (about 2 percent per year). It has the highest population density among the study areas (134 inhabitants per sq km), although still below the average for the Mezzogiorno. The population is relatively young and has a relatively high rate of literacy. Services are the most important non-agricultural activities; agriculture accounts for 15 percent of employment. Part time farming is common.

Average farm size is 10 ha (of cropland); as in the other zones, land is unequally distributed. Ten percent of the farms operate 62 percent of the total area. But in this zone, irrigation is relatively prominent, accounting for 13 percent of cropped area. Horticulture has grown in importance in recent years, but further expansion depends on increases in irrigated area. Irrigation is important also to permanent crops, especially vineyards and olive orchards. Eighty percent of the area is occupied by annual crops, mainly durum wheat. Livestock has little importance, but livestock farms are large compared to those in the other zones.

The representative farm systems

Identification of the representative farms considered holdings with an economic dimension between 4 and 100 EDU.[1] Farms outside this range were not of direct interest to this study. CAP measures are of little relevance to the very small farms; most of their production is intended for home consumption and their output accounts for only a trivial share of the family's income. The larger farms were excluded because of the study's focus on the problems of small farm agriculture. Farms in the 4-100 EDU class account for 17 percent of farms and 58 percent of agricultural area in Potenza; for Avellino, the respective figures are 21 and 57 percent; and for Campobasso-Foggia, 28 and 74 percent. If the farm population considered only commercially-oriented farms, the 4-100 EDU class would have heightened importance, with shares approximating those for agricultural area.

---

[1] EDU is the unit of economic dimension used by the EC Farm Accounting Network. 1 EDU represents a gross revenue of 1,200 ECU; in 1991, 1200 ECU equaled about 1.8 million lira.

Data were collected from the farms participating in the FADN (Farm Accounting Data Network) and from a field survey of a random sample of FADN farms. The sample was stratified according to location, dimension, and technical orientation. Sample size was 184: 57 farms in Alta Val d'Agri; 46 farms in Ufita-Alta Irpinia; and 81 farms in Basso Molise-Alta Capitanata. The data collected from the field survey included information about household characteristics, hired labor, parcel structure, potential change in parcels, ownership and tenure arrangements, cropping and livestock patterns and production technologies, a survey of capital equipment and stocks, and an historical review of changes in farm characteristics and the use of agricultural policy measures.

Information was organized into a database for statistical analysis. The information on family characteristics, structure of the farm, and cropping patterns was used in a principal components analysis to isolate the principal sources of variability and identify the variables most important for discriminating the data set. The most important variables were used in a subsequent cluster analysis to group the farms into homogeneous sets.

In the Alta Val d'Agri and Basso Molise-Alta Capitanata areas, the groups selected through the statistical analyses served to establish almost all characteristics of the representative farms. In Ufita-Alta Irpinia, the results did not appear so useful. Instead, the representative farms were established on the basis of ad hoc criteria, mainly farm size and location. In total, 20 clusters were chosen - 6 for Alta Val d'Agri, 6 for Ufita-Alta Irpinia, and 8 for Basso Molise-Alta Capitanata.

Alta Val d'Agri farming systems

On the basis of the six clusters considered for the Alta Val d'Agri zone, 7 representative farming systems were defined (Table 4.1). One cluster was divided into two representative farms because these farms demonstrated different choices in cropping patterns. Some of this group, primarily those with fewer available family workers, had abandoned livestock and specialized completely in crops.

All of the farm systems are family operations, usually between 10 and 20 ha in size. None of the farms participated in the rental market. Hired labor was uncommon, except for help in harvesting of horticultural crops. Cropping patterns correspond usually to available family labor supplies. Where labor was available and sufficiently young, livestock were a part of the farm operation. Five of the seven farm systems contain livestock - beef for meat, dairy cows, sheep, and goats are common in Val d'Agri. The sheep and goat activities have two principal outputs - lamb meat and cheese. Sheep cheese traditionally is made on the farm by women. The cheese has a well-established market; almost no markets exist for milk. All the farms with livestock produce forages; those without livestock give emphasis to cereals and horticultural crops. Occasionally, forage is produced for sale. Five of the farms have some irrigated area, and many have the potential to increase irrigated area beyond that currently used. The livestock farms often use irrigated area to produce forages. All the

Table 4.1
Alta Val d'Agri: features of the agriculture production system

	1. small mountain farm	2. small irrigated farm	3. large mountain farm	4.1. medium irrigated farm	4.2. small irrigated with dairy operation	5. small rainfed farm with livestock	6. small part-time farm
Crop land (Ha)	11.5	21	7	114	20	10	11
Rented area(%)	0	0	0	0	0	0	0
Irrigable area(%)(ha)	0	1	4	20	10	6	0
Irrigated area(% of total)	0	5	100	17.5	100	100	0
N° of plots	3	3	1	7	3	2	3
Average distance(Km)	3		0	2	1	0.5	2
N° of tractors(hours)	1(152)	1(170)	1(279)	2(1294)	1(613)	1(319)	1(103)
Total power(HP)	64	64	84	154	74	74	85
Prevalent activity							
Crops(ha)	durum wheat(2)	tomato(1) beans(1) durum wheat(3)		alfalfa(9) soft wheat(6) durum wheat(1)	durum wheat (2)	durum wheat(1)	durum wheat(3) soft wheat(2)
Livestock(head)	beef(5) sheep and goats(40)		beef(25) dairy(26) sheep and goats(70)		dairy(8) calves(6)	dairy(5) sheep and goats(40)	dairy(5)
Active Family Members:							
Total	2	2	2	1	2	2	2
Off-farm employed	0	0	0.5	0	0.5	0	1
On-farm employed: available UL	2	2	1.5	1	1.5	2	1
utilized UL(days)	1.47(422)	0.59(170)	1.38(396)	0.32(93)	0.82(237)	1.27(364)	0.92(263)

Source: Team estimates

farms have tractors, though most rely on the machinery service market for the provision of specialized services, such as harvesting.

Of the seven farm systems, three stand out as particularly different from the rest of the small farm population. One of the farms is particularly large, over 100 ha. Compared to the rest of the farms, this farm is well-endowed with machinery (two tractors instead of one, and more implements). It has 20 ha of irrigated area, for alfalfa and corn silage production. Livestock include beef, dairy cows, sheep, and goats. This farm family also participates in the off-farm labor market, both renting out their labor and hiring in farm labor. All land is owned. This farm is relatively large and on the verge of leaving the 'small farm' category. Off farm obligations of the family may create an upper limit on farm size.

The other two distinct farms are notable for their lack of irrigation. Both farms are about ten ha and demonstrate two different production strategies. One cohort has remained specialized in livestock production, mainly dairy and calves. Another group has become part-time farms. Similarly endowed in agricultural and demographic characteristics, they have joined the off farm labor market and produce grains as well as fodder for animals. Farm labor demands thus are somewhat less than those of the full time farm. The full time farm has specialized in dairy cows, giving up sheep production because the time requirements are too stringent.

Ufita-Alta Irpinia farming systems

Six farming systems were identified for this region, three in each of the sub-zones (Table 4.2). Three farm systems are used to represent small farming in Ufita, one located in the level valley land and two in the more prominent mountainous terrain. The systems range from 5 to 12 ha. Each of the farms is comprised of four parcels, usually located quite close to the farm center. The land rental market is active, and two of the systems rent in land. The farm in the valley has about a fourth of its area devoted to irrigated crops (tobacco). The other systems are entirely rainfed. All farms are equipped with a tractor, and the irrigated system also has a diesel pump to pump well water.

The systems have similar cropping patterns. Tobacco is the dominant crop in this sub-zone, and all farms produce some. Durum wheat and forages are also grown. If animals are not part of the farm system, forage production is marketed. The smaller mountainous farm (5 ha) raises tobacco on a fourth of the area, the remainder being devoted to cereals (durum wheat and barley), forages, and about 0.5 ha of permanent crops (olives and vineyards). Beef are raised on the largest farm (12 ha), along with cereals (4.7 ha of durum wheat and 2.2 ha of barley), forages, and rainfed tobacco. Forage is used on the farm for the cattle.

Systems in Alta Irpinia are oriented toward livestock and cereals. Milk and beef are the main products. Farms differ mainly in size. Three representative farms are used to model this area, ranging in size from 6 to 35 ha. Herd sizes are as large as 20 head. As in Ufita, farms may be comprised of a large number of parcels, but these usually are located near the farm center and transport is not too onerous. Larger farms are generally better endowed with machinery, such as

71

Table 4.2
Ufita-Alta Irpinia: features of the farm systems

	Irrigated Tobacco Ufita	Rainfed Tobacco Ufita	Traditional Ufita	Small Traditional Alta Irpinia	Medium Traditional Alta Irpinia	Large Traditional Alta Irpinia
	valley		mountainous			
Crop land (Ha)	8.4	4.93	11.8	6.19	18	35
Rented area(%)	15	0	36.5	0	8.3	0
Irrigable area(ha)	2	0	0	0	0	0
Irrigated area(%)	23.2	0	0	0	0	0
N° of plots	4	4	4	4	8	5
Average distance(Km)	1	2	0.5	0.5	1	1.2
N° of tractors	1	1	1	1	1	2
Total power(HP)	109	70	90	70	95	150
Prevalent activity						
Crops(ha)	tobacco(1.95) durum wheat(3.65)	tobacco(1.05) durum wheat(1.5)	tobacco(1.33) durum wheat(4.69)	soft wheat(1.14) durum wheat(4)	durum wheat(4)	durum wheat(8.65)
Livestock(head)			beef(4)	dairy(4)	dairy(14)	dairy(20) sheep(45)
Active Family Members:						
Total	2	2	2	3	2	2
Off-farm employed	0	1	0	1	0	0
On-farm employed: available UL	2	1.23	2	2.17	2	2.19
utilized UL(days)	1.30(374)	0.64(155)	1.24(357)	1.10(316)	1.54(443)	2.19(630)

Note: 1UL= 2.300 hours
Source: Farm Survey

forage harvesting equipment. All farms rely on family labor, absorbing as much as 2 years of labor per farm, and all family members are involved in the farm. Only the smallest farm (6 ha) participates in the off-farm labor market.

Basso Molise-Alta Capitanata farming systems

A much different agriculture is represented in Basso Molise and Alta Capitanata. Cluster analysis was used to define 8 farming systems for the Basso Molise-Alta Capitanata zone (Table 4.3). Systems range from 6 to 80 ha in size, but most of the systems (six) are between 10 and 18 ha. This area is flourishing economically, and the farm systems are more lucrative, labor extensive, and capital intensive than those in the other study areas. Farm families are relatively young. Three of the systems have family members working off-farm, and on-farm employment of the farms is almost always less than one FTE (full time equivalent). For most of the systems, irrigated area is between one-fourth and two-thirds of the cultivated area. If water were available, irrigated area would be even larger. All land is owner-operated.

As might be expected, many of the farm systems are specialized in permanent crops (wine grapes or fruit) or horticulture. One farm is 14 ha, with half the area in peaches. The 10 ha non-demarcated (non-DOC) vineyard system has 90 percent of the area in grapes. The other vineyard system is 18 ha, in a DOC area, and has 80 percent of the area in grapes. The 15.5 ha system, the most common farm type in the sample, is more diversified, but all area is in specialty crops - vineyards, peaches, olives, and horticulture. Other farms have chosen to remain in crops, producing cereals and industrial crops (sugarbeets and tomatoes for processing). One 12 ha system produces a three-year rotation of two wheat crops followed by horticulture, such as artichokes or fennel. Hired labor is common, especially for harvesting and pruning activities.

Exceptions to this characterization include the small, rainfed farm (6 ha), a part-time operation with one small tractor, producing cereals (durum wheat is cropped on three-fourths of the area). Vineyards and olives account for the remaining area and are used for home consumption. At the other extreme is a large farm (79 ha), with three irrigable parcels, four tractors, and full employment for the owner-operator. This farm produces cereals and industrial crops in a three-year rotation.

Representativeness of the farm systems

The representativeness of the farm systems in the four provinces, measured in terms of technical orientation (OTE) and economic dimension (EDU), is summarized in Table 4.4. The farm systems represent about 45 percent of the total number of farms (considering only those farms between 4 and 100 EDU) and about 62 percent of the cultivated area. The 21 farm systems considered here thus represent a substantial portion of small farm agriculture in a very diverse sector. The principal types of farms not considered in this study are classified in the OTE system as horticulture, pigs and poultry, or mixed livestock. But a good indication of horticultural and livestock potentials is

Table 4.3
Basso Molise-Alta Capitanata: features of the farm systems

	1. Fruit-growing	2. Medium non-DOC vine-growing	3. Mixed	4. Industrial crop	5. Small dry rainfed	6. Large DOC vine-growing	7. Medium cereals, vegetable	8. Large mixed
Crop land (Ha)	14	9.5	15.5	10.8	6.5	18	12	79
Rented area(%)	0	0	0	0	0	0	0	0
Irrigated area(ha)	9.5	3.5	7.5	5.8	0	5	4	29
Irrigable area(%)	100	100	100	100	0	100	100	100
No of plots	3	2	3	2	2	3	3	3
Average distance(Km)	0.1	0.1	0.1	0.1	0	7	0.2	0.5
No of tractors	2	2	2	1	1	2	2	4
Total power(HP)	130	130	110	60	60	130	210	370
Prevalent activity:								
Crops(ha)	peach(7) durum wheat(4) sunflower(2.5)	vineyard(7) peach(1) durum wheat(1)	vineyard(4) durum wheat(4) sugar beet(2.5)	sugar beet(3.5) durum wheat(2.5) vineyard(2.5) tomato(1.8)	durum wheat(5) vineyard(1)	vineyard(15) olive(3)	durum wheat(8) fennel(4) artichoke(4)	durum wheat(41) sugar beet(20) tomato(5)
Active Family Members:								
Total	4	3	2	3	3	3	3	1
Off-farm employed	1	0	0	1	1	0	0	0
On-farm employed: available UL	1.9	2.8	1.4	1.6	1.7	2.4	1.7	1
utilized UL(days)	0.68(194)	0.86(246)	0.79(227)	0.66(190)	0.35(99)	1.31(378)	0.72(208)	1.00(288)

Note: 1UL=2.300 hours
Source: Farm Survey

Table 4.4
Representativeness of the farming systems

General OTE	Class of UDE*	Representative Farming system	Representativeness** % of farms	Representativeness** % of cropland
Field crops — Alta Val d'Agri, Ufita-Alta Irpinia, Basso Molise-Alta Capitanata	4-8	4.1, Med. irrigated, Rainfed tobacco, 5, Small rainfed	13.9	8.0
Field crops — Alta Val d'Agri, Ufita-Alta Irpinia	8-16	2, Small irrigated	9.0	9.7
Field crops — Basso Molise-Alta Capitanata	16-40	Irrigated tobacco, Traditional 4,7, Industrial	5.0	12.7
Field crops — Basso Molise-Alta Capitanata	40-100	8, Large	1.3	7.5
Permanent crops — Basso Molise-Alta Capitanata	16-40	1,2,6	6.0	6.3
Grazing livestock — Alta Val d'Agri	4-8	1,4,2,5	2.4	2.2
Grazing livestock — Alta Val d'Agri	16-40	3	1.0	3.8
Mixed cropping — Basso Molise-Alta Capitanata	16-40	3	1.7	3.1
Grazing livestock — Alta Val d'Agri, Ufita-Alta Irpinia	4-8	6	2.6	2.4
Crops-livestock — Ufita-Alta Irpinia	8-16	Small Traditional Alta Irpinia, Medium Traditional Alta Irpinia	1.5	2.9
Crops-livestock — Ufita-Alta Irpinia	16-40	Large Traditional Alta Irpinia	0.8	3.5
Total			45.3	62.1

* 1 UDE=1.200 ECU

** Considers only UDE 4-100 in provinces of Avellino, Potenza, Foggia, and Campobasso.

Source: ISTAT Agricultural Census, 1990.

75

captured by the systems already included and by the simulations of potential changes. Some of the permanent crop farms, usually growing vineyards or olives, also are considered only partly in these farm models. But the omissions are relatively minor. Consultations with expert observers confirmed that the data set provides a comprehensive view of small farm agriculture in these areas of southern Italy. Agriculture in the rest of south Italy is quite another matter, of course. Other farm types, cropping patterns, and agro-ecological zones would be needed to cover this extraordinarily diverse agriculture.

Most of the representative systems (8) fall into the OTE category of field crops. Each of the regions contains substantial numbers of these types of farms in the four provinces. Field crop farms account for 29 percent of the farms and 38 percent of the area in the 4-100 EDU size class. Farms that are less obvious in the list of representative farms emerge as prominent elements in the small farm population - the small, rainfed farm in Basso Molise, the rainfed systems in the mountainous parts of Alta Irpinia, and the small and medium irrigated farms of Val d'Agri. These farms would be the most obvious small farms to observers of the agricultural landscape in the study areas. The results show the skewed distribution of land, even within the small farm category. The large Basso Molise system (79 ha), for example, represents only one percent of the farms, but 8 percent of the area.

The 'crops-livestock' category is especially common in Alta Irpinia and in total includes 5 percent of the number of small farms and 9 percent of the cropland. Livestock systems are most prominent in Alta Val d'Agri, and in total this type of farm accounts for 5 percent of small farms and about 9 percent of area. The remaining category of small farms included in the sample is specialized in permanent crops. The three representative systems, all in the Basso Molise-Alta Capitanata area, account for only 5 percent of the farms and less than ten percent of the small farm area in the study region.

Baseline economic results

Farm models were used to evaluate the economic performance of the farm systems. Crop and livestock budgets were constructed from technical coefficients to represent input requirements and farm gate prices. The budget data were gathered from secondary information, supplemented with information obtained during the field surveys in the three zones.

Baseline results represent the incentive structure of 1991, a relatively stable year (Table 4.5). Ufita-Alta Irpinia emerges clearly as the poorest region among those surveyed. Returns are as low as Lira 6,000 per day (about US$4 per day) on the smallest traditional farm in Alta Irpinia. Returns are higher on the larger farms, but even the largest farm offers average daily returns that are only Lira 55,000, about a third higher than the unskilled daily wage rate in that region (Lira 40,000 per day). The other two regions show much wider variation and considerably more prosperity than the Ufita- Alta Irpinia zone. Low returns occur in Basso Molise in the small rainfed system and in the medium lower

Table 4.5
Economic results for Southern Italy farm systems, base year (1991)

System	Revenues	Total costs				Returns	Returns/day
		Intermediate Inputs	Capital	Land	Hired Labor		
		Lira					
VAL D'AGRI							
1. Small mountain	42,280,519	8,371,997	6,291,837	2,282,000	0	25,334,685	60,088
2. Small irrigated	45,514,871	6,624,319	7,974,739	1,218,000	7,331,878	22,365,935	131,371
3. Large mountain	180,942,994	41,313,431	33,980,381	16,210,000	22,097,779	67,341,404	170,252
4.1. Med. irrigated	36,042,145	12,502,984	9,005,364	3,480,000	465,217	10,588,580	113,398
4.2. Small irrig. w/dairy	46,923,914	13,266,013	10,766,141	1,740,000	0	21,151,760	89,437
5. Small rainfed w/livestock	38,444,002	8,841,759	7,140,604	1,620,000	0	20,841,639	57,257
6. Small part-time	28,619,944	5,561,807	5,690,364	1,756,000	0	15,611,774	59,276
UFITA-ALTA IRPINIA							
1. Irrig. tobacco	32,275,624	5,204,789	4,872,073	3,691,260	270,556	18,236,946	48,795
2. Rainfed tobacco	15,394,951	2,856,652	3,599,344	1,308,660	147,096	7,483,198	48,201
3. Ufita traditional	33,243,207	9,250,183	5,109,382	2,845,180	286,951	15,751,511	44,184
4. Alta Irpinia small trad.	15,148,618	7,201,590	3,936,539	1,699,960	292,425	2,018,105	6,381
5. Alta Irpinia med. trad.	51,531,111	19,470,530	9,624,536	4,194,640	785,545	17,455,860	39,426
6. Alta Irpinia large trad.	85,775,970	28,669,698	13,285,884	7,829,380	1,096,930	34,894,078	55,420
BASSO MOLISE							
1. Fruit	83,744,865	13,424,811	30,617,559	5,040,000	15,153,278	19,509,217	100,427
2. Med non-DOC wine	52,012,294	9,579,820	24,308,426	3,420,000	7,520,210	7,183,838	29,172
3. Mixed	75,103,962	17,146,534	20,251,778	5,580,000	10,159,255	21,966,395	96,897
4. Industrial crops	65,305,807	15,429,945	12,684,262	3,888,000	7,518,102	25,785,497	135,539
5. Small rainfed	16,085,225	4,669,951	6,859,496	2,340,000	0	2,215,778	22,314
6. Large DOC wine	92,159,651	15,123,618	28,085,647	6,480,000	22,825,485	19,644,901	52,036
7. Med. cereals/vegetable	71,888,787	19,195,853	20,448,991	4,320,000	4,323,363	23,600,580	113,492
8. Large mixed	311,731,235	73,446,083	58,144,684	28,440,000	42,383,970	109,316,499	380,231

Source: Team estimates

quality wine system, on the order of Lira 20,000-30,000 per day.

The other systems offer returns to family labor that are at least Lira 50,000 per day, and the more prosperous systems offer returns that are two or three times that level. Systems that have introduced industrial crops, such as sugar beets or tomatoes, or fruits and vegetables earned comfortable returns to family labor. Irrigated farms generally did better than rainfed farms, and the relatively larger farms usually offered higher returns than the small farms (although the presence of irrigation could offset this tendency; the small, irrigated farm in Val d'Agri offers among the highest returns in that zone).

The results show also that most of the economically successful small farm systems are capital- and intermediate input intensive. In almost all of the systems, these two categories of inputs account for three-fourths or more of non-family input costs. In terms of capital intensity, the Ufita- Alta Irpinia zone again stands in stark contrast to the others. Annual capital expenditures of small farms in Val d'Agri and Basso Molise are often more than 10 million Lira and sometimes much more. In Ufita- Alta Irpinia, this category of expenditures is less than 5 million Lira for all but the two largest farm systems. Hired labor costs are most substantial for the vegetable, fruit, and wine systems. Land costs (most often an opportunity cost, given the low level of activity in the land rental market) are relatively unimportant. They were rarely more than 15 percent of costs. They were largest when irrigated land was involved.

Results are aggregated in Table 4.6, to represent the net incentive pattern for small farms in the four provinces studied. The rates of return used to measure competitiveness were based on the wage rates of unskilled laborers in the agriculture and construction sectors - 10 million Lira per year for Val d'Agri and Ufita-Alta Irpinia, and 13.5 million Lira for Basso Molise-Alta Capitanata. These amounts translate to about 40,000 and 54,000 Lira per day, respectively ($US 27 and 36). These benchmarks favor the finding of competitiveness; for farmers with higher opportunity costs for their labor (medium skill wages, for example, were about 24 million Lira), the characterization of competitiveness may be insufficient to retain resources in agriculture. On the other hand, where access to off-farm labor markets is less than perfect, the opportunity cost measures overstate the necessary rates of return.

In total, 17 of the 21 systems were competitive in 1991-92; family labor was remunerated at a level comparable to that offered by (unskilled) off farm employment. This condition prevailed in all three zones. Assuming the representativeness of the considered farming systems pertains also for the other small farm systems in the four provinces, the competitive systems represented about 65 percent of the small farms in the region and more than 80 percent of the cropped area. Only one of the systems - an Ufita system accounting for 2 percent of farms and a trivial portion of total area - appeared non-competitive in the short run. Only these farms could be considered truly 'stuck' in the agricultural sector, able to increase incomes only if they could escape the agricultural sector. More systems - two in Basso Molise and one in Val d'Agri (accounting for one third of farms and 20 percent of area) - were not competitive in the long run and thus had incentive to leave the sector after fixed assets could be depreciated and liquidated. But in general, small farm agriculture of the

Table 4.6
Competitiveness of Southern Italy farming systems in 1991-92

Types of Systems	No of Systems				% of No of Farms				% of Arable land			
	Val d'Agri	Ufita	Basso Molise	Total	Val d'Agri	Ufita	Basso Molise	Total	Val d'Agri	Ufita	Basso Molise	Total
Competitive without direct support	6	3	5	14	15.1	5.1	34.1	54.2	17.1	4.7	53.7	75.5
Competitive only with direct support	0	2	1	3	0.0	10.3	0.2	10.5	0.0	4.7	0.7	5.4
Non-Competitive but viable in the short run	1	0	2	3	3.4	0.0	29.6	33.0	3.2	1.2	14.7	19.1
Non-Competitive and non-viable	0	1	0	1	0.0	2.3	0.0	2.3	0.0	0.0	0.0	0.0
TOTAL	7	6	8	21	18.4	17.7	63.9	100.0	20.3	10.6	69.1	100.0

Source: Team estimates

79

early 1990s in this part of southern Italy was competitive and well-adjusted to prevailing economic incentives.

Table 4.6 shows that direct subsidies were a relatively unimportant factor in generating competitiveness. Only 3 of the systems required direct subsidies to reach a competitive rate of return. Subsidies were most important in Ufita-Alta Irpinia, where 2 of the 3 competitive systems depended on direct subsidies. This result is a consequence of the prominence of durum wheat in the representative systems of this zone and the payment of a special subsidy for this crop. Still, these farms represent only 10 percent of the population and 5 percent of small farm area.

The most profitable systems are the farms with livestock and irrigated crops in Val d'Agri, the large mountain livestock system in Val d'Agri, and the vegetable, fruit, and industrial crop systems of Basso Molise-Alta Capitanata. The least profitable systems were concentrated in the Ufita-Alta Irpinia zone. Even though this region is the poorest studied and opportunity costs for labor were relatively low, farm systems were not competitive. Especially low returns were found in the small and large traditional systems and the rainfed tobacco system; profits were low also in the small mountain and rainfed livestock systems in Val d'Agri, and the small rainfed and non-DOC vineyard systems of Basso Molise-Alta Capitanata.

The impact of CAP reform and possible change in crop mix and technologies

Future competitiveness was analyzed in three steps. First, the team researchers identified the expected changes in Italian agricultural output, input, and domestic factor prices and income supports, projected to the complete implementation of CAP reform and the appearance of long run equilibrium in market incentives. Next, the new price and subsidy system was introduced to the farm model to estimate returns to family labor. These results are termed the 'projected baseline.' Finally, possible changes in crop mix and technologies were identified. Introduction of these changes into the projected baseline generates the 'potential economic results.' They are considered to be potential because they presume adjustments on the part of farmers.

The effects of the CAP reform

The economic results associated with the CAP reform are presented in Table 4.7. The results are presented for the total area studied (four provinces in south Italy) and for each of the zones. The effects of MacSharry reforms and other long-run adjustments in the economy are minor. CAP reform will reduce the number of competitive systems from 17 to 14; the prominence of farm numbers declines from 65 percent to 60 percent; and the share of cropped area that appears competitive declines from 81 to 74 percent. The intent of MacSharry reforms - to alter the structure of market incentives without affecting adversely the incomes of farmers - seems largely satisfied.

80

Table 4.7
Southern Italy baseline and projected competitiveness
(without crop mix or technological changes)

	Baseline prices			Projected prices		
Totals	No of systems	% No of farms	% Arable land	No of systems	% No of farms	% Arable land
Competitive without direct support	14	54.2	75.5	5	30.0	52.7
Competitive only with direct support	3	10.5	5.4	9	29.8	21.7
Non-Competitive but viable in the short run	3	33.0	19.1	5	34.5	21.2
Non-Competitive and non-viable	1	2.3	0.0	2	5.7	4.4
TOTAL	21	100.0	100.0	21	100.0	100.0
Val d'Agri						
Competitive without direct support	6	81.5	84.2	3	34.8	39.4
Competitive only with direct support	0	0.0	0.0	2	44.0	30.5
Non-Competitive but viable in the short run	1	18.5	15.8	1	2.7	14.3
Non-Competitive and non-viable	0	0.0	0.0	1	18.5	15.8
TOTAL	7	100.0	100.0	7	100.0	100.0
Ufita-Alta Irpinia						
Competitive without direct support	3	28.8	44.3	0	0.0	0.0
Competitive only with direct support	2	58.2	44.4	3	62.1	54.7
Non-Competitive but viable in the short run	0	0.0	11.3	2	24.9	34.0
Non-Competitive and non-viable	1	13.0	0.0	1	13.0	11.3
TOTAL	6	100.0	100.0	6	100.0	100.0
Basso-Molise						
Competitive without direct support	5	53.4	77.7	2	36.9	64.7
Competitive only with direct support	1	1.3	1.1	4	16.8	14.0
Non-Competitive but viable in the short run	2	46.3	21.2	2	46.3	21.3
Non-Competitive and non-viable	0	0.0	0.0	0	0.0	0.0
TOTAL	8	100.0	100.0	8	100.0	100.0

Source: Team estimates

Incomes decline somewhat, but the declines are small (on the order of 5 to 10 percent), and the magnitudes usually are not large enough to alter the competitive status of farm systems. The number of noncompetitive systems increases from 4 to 7. These farms are the relatively small farms, usually located in rainfed and hilly areas. Noncompetitive farms account for 40 percent of the population but only 26 percent of the cultivated area.

More noticeable effects of reform are the changes in types of policy assistance. Support to farmers become much more obvious under the MacSharry reforms. Direct supports become much more important to the competitive systems that remain. Nine systems become dependent on direct supports for their competitive status, making up 30 percent of the farms and 22 percent of the cultivated area. This change reflects the substitution of direct support measures for market price supports. If political support weakens for this level of support, non-competitiveness will become a much more substantial problem. Pressure for structural change - outmigration of population and reshuffling of the farm sizes - would become much more noticeable.

The results for each zone show that the most substantial adjustments come in Val d'Agri and Ufita-Alta Irpinia. Most or all of the competitive systems that remain become dependent on direct supports. The importance of direct supports increases also in the Basso Molise-Alta Capitanata zone, but they still account for less than half the number of representative systems and less than 20 percent of the cultivated area. The largest declines in profitability from CAP reform are suffered by the livestock systems - the mountain systems and the small dairy and medium irrigated systems in Val d'Agri. In Ufita-Alta Irpinia, the most affected systems are irrigated tobacco and the traditional diversified system. In Basso Molise, the small rainfed, the non-DOC vineyard, fruit, and the medium cereals and vegetable systems suffer the biggest reductions in profits. Both the reductions in CAP prices and the price declines associated with introduction of the single market regulation have negative effects on profitability.

Simulation of possible changes in crop mixes and technologies

The marked changes in policy will bring dramatic changes in incentives, and farmers are not going to sit by idly while profits decline. Nor are they likely to give up on agriculture easily and abandon it in favor of other pursuits. But prediction of the changes that will occur is difficult. Projections of the effects of particular supply elasticities for expected output and input price changes is difficult given available data and undoubtedly inaccurate given the substantial magnitudes of change anticipated.

Evaluations of response focused on the economic effects of potential changes in crop mix and technologies. The attempt here was to identify potential changes that could be applied to the larger share of the population - transformations of representative farms into the 'new' representative farms of the post-MacSharry era. This focused the research effort on particular changes that could be potentially implemented in each of the regions.

The simulations for Val d'Agri are based mainly on changes in the livestock activities. Given the sharp declines in the profitability of beef production, these systems are expected to disappear from the area. Dairy systems also will experience some pressure, depending on final decisions about allocation of milk quotas. Regional markets would favor the local dairy systems. Implementation of a national market in trade of quota rights is expected to favor northern producers. New technologies suitable to local conditions are not known, and the small farm sizes and relatively high local costs of production of feeds will make difficult the continuation of these activities.

The considered changes in farm systems are described in Figure 4.1. Changes in the two dairy farms - the small irrigated farm with dairy, and the small rainfed farm with livestock - are increases in the number of dairy cows to get the benefits of a larger scale of milk production. Because these animals substitute for beef animals, the farm is not required to increase forage production or to purchase feeds. In both systems, purchase of quota rights will be necessary to allow an increase in milk production. These should be obtainable if the quota market is allowed to function at a local level. Examples of possible sellers of quota include older dairy farmers interested in the early retirement program.

The two mountain systems - small and large mountain beef farms - were altered by substituting beef with sheep and goat production. The remaining three systems - small and medium irrigated and small part-time farms - were assumed to eliminate beef production (if present) but also to introduce new production activities. Strawberries and soft wheat were introduced to the small irrigated farm, apples and beans were simulated on the medium irrigated farm, and irrigated beans were introduced to the small part-time farm. The regional extension services consider these crops especially appropriate for the zone, and no technical problems are expected to hinder production. The more difficult constraints to increased production will involve the development of post-farm treatment and marketing networks for these specialty crops.

In the Ufita-Alta Irpinia zone, the simulations emphasized reductions in the scale of machinery and equipment and changes in crop mix (Figure 4.2). Machinery stocks had been built up because of the substantial subsidy programs of the 1980s, and elimination of these subsidy programs in the 1990s is expected to encourage farmers to become more parsimonious in their use of equipment. Reduction of the machinery stock in the large traditional system caused fixed costs to decline from 33 to 29 percent of total revenue. For the medium and large traditional Alta Irpinia systems, the main crop mix change was to remove durum wheat in favor of increased forage production; this change allowed farms to introduce sheep production.

But the big crop changes in this zone will involve tobacco, where CAP reform will introduce strict limits on European production. For the irrigated tobacco system, the simulation reduces tobacco area by 44 percent in response to the introduction of the quota for dark, air-cured tobacco. The tobacco area was substituted with three horticultural crops - aubergine (eggplant), peppers, and potatoes. These crops are well adapted to agro-climatic conditions; marketing networks exist already for these commodities. A similar reduction in tobacco was simulated for the rainfed tobacco system, and the available land area was assumed to be planted to olives and garlic. Introduction of olives has been favored by a regional development program to expand olive production in

Systems	Production with new activities	
	livestock and crop variation	crop variation
1. Small mountain farm	X	
2. Small irrigated farm		X
3. Large mountain farm	X	
4.1. Medium irrigated farm		X
4.2. Small irrigated with dairy operation	X	
5. Small rainfed with livestock	X	
6. Small part-time		X

Figure 4.1 Modifications of farm systems in Alta Val d'Agri

Systems	Machinery reduction	Production with new activities	
		crop variation	livestock and crop variation
1. Irrigated tobacco		X	
2. Rainfed tobacco		X	
3. Traditional Ufita		X	
4. Small traditional Alta Irpinia			
5. Medium traditional Alta Irpinia			X
6. Large traditional Alta Irpinia	X		X

Figure 4.2 Modifications applied to systems in Ufita-Alta Irpinia

the region; the program provides capital and interest rate subsidies. The simulation of garlic production was stimulated by a recent effort of marketing agents to expand garlic production. This expansion is a response to reduction in production in other zones of Campania, such as the Sele Valley, where urbanization has converted much agricultural land. In the traditional Ufita system, rainfed tobacco area was substituted by garlic and forages. Increased forage production allowed this farm system to increase its degree of self-sufficiency in livestock feed.

In the Basso Molise-Alta Capitanata zone, the simulations emphasized reduction in the capital stock and changes in crop mix (Figure 4.3). The region faces few agro-climatic, technological, or marketing constraints to the introduction of new crops, and farms have probably the greatest flexibility in choice among all the zones. Simulations of change thus are the most arbitrary of the simulations. The simulations concentrated on maintaining a wide diversity of cropping options. Two of the systems - small rainfed and medium non-DOC wine - only reduced their capital stock. Two other systems - industrial crops and large mixed crop farms - considered only changes in crop mix. The industrial crop farm system introduces an annual cereal crop for sugar beet and tomatoes and substitutes peaches and plums for the non-DOC vineyard. The simulation for the large mixed farm removed vineyards in favor of expansion of the existing rainfed crop rotation.

Both changes - new crop mixes and reductions in capital stock - were introduced in the remaining farm systems. For the fruit-growing system, reduction in machinery inputs caused a decline in the share of fixed costs in total revenue, from 47 to 40 percent. The principal crop substitutions were plums substituted for the non-DOC vineyard. The share of fixed costs in the mixed farming system declined from 36 to 32 percent of total revenue; sugar beets and tomato areas were expanded, and onions and peas were introduced to replace sunflower and the non-DOC vineyards. For the large DOC vineyard, improved varieties were introduced (Trebbiano and Montepulciano for Bombino), resulting in higher output prices; greater efficiency in machinery use caused the share of fixed costs in total revenue to decline from 36 to 32 percent. In the medium cereal and vegetable system, the cereal-vegetable area was reduced in favor of tomato and sugar beets; fixed cost shares declined from 38 to 26 percent.

Introduction of budgets for the new activities into the farm models made possible the estimation of expected returns to farm labor. The results (Table 4.8) show that further crop substitution and technical change in these regions would allow the present level of competitiveness to be maintained after introduction of the CAP reforms. The changes increase competitive status to 68 percent of the farms and 84 percent of the area. Without farm changes, only 60 percent of farms and 75 percent of the area are competitive. The other notable effect is that exposure of farms to CAP subsidies diminishes. Dependence on subsidies for competitiveness decreases by about half, from 22 to 11 percent of the cropped area. This shift reflects the marked reduction in CAP crop area for many of the simulations. This result highlights also the importance of development of markets for new specialty crops, such as garlic and strawberries.

Systems	Machinery reduction	Production with new activities — with crop variation
1. Fruit	X	X
2. Medium non-DOC wine	X	
3. Mixed	X	X
4. Industrial crop		X
5. Small rainfed	X	
6. Large DOC wine	X	X
7. Medium cereals, vegetables	X	X
8. Large mixed	X	X

Figure 4.3 Modifications applied to systems in Basso Molise-Alta Capitanata

Table 4.8
Southern Italy* projected competitiveness with change

Totals	Projected prices, without crop mix and/or technological changes			Projected prices, with crop mix and/or technological changes		
	No of systems	% No of farms	% Arable land	No of systems	% No of farms	% Arable land
Competitive without direct support	5	30.0	52.7	13	51.1	73.5
Competitive only with direct support	9	29.8	21.7	5	17.0	10.6
Non-Competitive but viable in the short run	5	34.5	21.2	2	29.6	14.7
Non-Competitive and non-viable	2	5.7	4.4	1	2.3	1.2
TOTAL	21	100.0	100.0	21	100.0	100.0
Val d'Agri						
Competitive without direct support	3	34.8	39.4	6	81.5	84.2
Competitive only with direct support	2	44.0	30.5	1	18.5	15.8
Non-Competitive but viable in the short run	1	2.7	14.3	0	0.0	0.0
Non-Competitive and non-viable	1	18.5	15.8	0	0.0	0.0
TOTAL	7	100.0	100.0	7	100.0	100.0
Ufita						
Competitive without direct support	0	0.0	0.0	2	11.3	25.5
Competitive only with direct support	3	62.1	54.7	3	75.7	63.2
Non-Competitive but viable in the short run	2	24.9	34.0	0	0.0	0.0
Non-Competitive and non-viable	1	13.0	11.3	1	13.0	11.3
TOTAL	6	100.0	100.0	7	100.0	100.0
Basso-Molise-Alta Capitanata						
Competitive without direct support	2	36.9	64.7	5	53.4	77.7
Competitive only with direct support	4	16.8	14.0	1	0.3	15.8
Non-Competitive but viable in the short run	2	46.3	21.3	2	46.3	21.3
Non-Competitive and non-viable	0	0.0	0.0	0	0.0	0.0
TOTAL	8	100.0	100.0	8	100.0	100.0

Source: Team estimates

*Southern Italy here refers only to provinces of Avellino, Potenza, Foggia and Campobasso

For most of the Val d'Agri systems, the results show improvement in competitiveness not only with respect to the projected baseline, but also with respect to the pre-MacSharry (1991-92) baseline. All the Val d'Agri systems are competitive, and only the part-time system remains dependent on direct supports. Rates of return in Ufita-Alta Irpinia improve considerably. The number of competitive systems increases to the levels of the pre-MacSharry baseline. The simulation results for Basso Molise-Alta Capitanata also show improvements in competitiveness. These improvements are less marked than in the other two zones, highlighting the relative stability of the expected economic performance of the Basso Molise-Alta Capitanata systems.

The importance of change for future competitiveness is summarized in Table 4.9. Most of the systems (14 of 21) will be able to compete in the future even without further changes in crop mix and technology. These systems represent about 60 percent of the total number of farms and about 75 percent of the total cultivated area in the regions. The largest number of competitive farms and the largest share of cultivated area are located in the Basso Molise-Alta Capitanata region. Four of the systems are potentially competitive with the simulated changes in crop mix and technologies; these systems account for 8 percent of farms and 9 percent of total area and are located mostly in Val d'Agri and Ufita-Alta Irpinia. On the less optimistic side, more than 30 percent of the farms and 16 percent of the area are not competitive with the simulated changes; these farms are particularly prominent in the Ufita-Alta Irpinia zone. For these farms, further changes are essential to long run viability. Without these, as yet unknown, changes, outmigration from agriculture seems inevitable. The survival of agriculture will presumably depend on larger farms.

Implications for structural change

The extent of structural adjustment of rural areas in these parts of southern Italy and the policies needed to ease the process of structural adjustment are the principal concerns of national policy makers. Non-competitive systems will be expected eventually to release their farm population to alternative off farm employment. But some of the competitive systems may also face difficulties. Systems that offer competitive rates of return but small total employment may find also that on farm employment can not be sustained, particularly if they are located in areas with inflexible labor and land markets. Farmers in these systems will tend to leave agriculture, not because the rate of return to their resources is too small, but because their total remuneration is not comparable to what can be earned off the farm. They would desire to increase their farm size or find off farm employment for at least some of the family labor force, but in areas where this is not possible, emigration becomes the only solution. The third group of farms involved in structural change will include potentially competitive systems that are able to increase in size. These opportunities should arise in all areas as outmigration from agriculture makes land resources available to those who remain in the sector.

Most farms (68 percent of the number of farms and 84 percent of arable land) should be classified as autonomous or potentially autonomous, offering at least

89

Table 4.9
Change and future competitiveness of Southern Italy* farming systems

System	Val d'Agri			Ufita-Alta Irpinia			Basso-Molise- Alta-Capitanata			TOTAL		
	No of systems	% No of farms	% Arable land	No of systems	% No of farms	% Arable land	No of systems	% No of farms	% Arable land	No of systems	% No of farms	% Arable land
Competitive	5	14.5	14.2	3	11.0	5.8	6	34.3	54.4	14	59.8	74.4
Potentially Competitive	2	3.9	6.1	2	4.4	3.6	0	0.0	0.0	4	8.3	9.7
Non-Competitive	0	0.0	0.0	1	2.3	1.2	2	29.6	14.7	3	31.9	15.9
TOTAL	7	18.4	20.3	6	17.7	10.6	8	63.9	69.1	21	100.0	100.0

Source: Team estimates
*Southern Italy here refers only to provinces of Avellino, Potenza, Foggia and Campobasso

one full-time equivalent in employment (Table 4.10). The non-autonomous systems (32 percent of the number of farms and 16 percent of cultivated area) correspond exclusively to the non-competitive category. Since these farms will not be viable, their exit from the agricultural sector appears inevitable.

In terms of absorption of available family labor, almost one half of the systems, representing 47 percent of the number of farms, will not be large enough or labor intensive enough to absorb the available family labor supply (Table 4.10). Most of the remaining systems (8 of 11 systems, representing 45 percent of the farms and 50 percent of cultivated area) will require changes in crop mix and technologies to absorb their family labor supplies. These farm families must accommodate an unusually large amount of leisure time or find additional employment - off the farm or through an increase in farm size.

Only 3 of the farming systems (8 percent of farm numbers and 22 percent of area) will avoid structural adjustment or changes in crop mix and technologies (Table 4.11). About 60 percent of farms and cultivated area will require significant adjustment to accommodate the effects of the new CAP policies and still remain in agriculture. For the competitive and potentially competitive parts of small farm agriculture, crop and technology changes have more importance than structural adjustment. Only 9 percent of farms and 7 percent of cultivated area depend exclusively on increases in farm size or off farm employment. About 60 percent of the farms will need to adjust their crop mix and technology to remain viable, and about 7 percent will need to adjust simultaneously both their crop mix and their farm size.

The structural adjustment implications of the results are significant. About 32 percent of farms and 16 percent of the area corresponds to farms that are non-viable; these farms will be expected eventually to supply land to the market for agricultural use and labor to the off farm labor market. Most of the viable and potentially viable farms also will have at least a possible interest in the factor markets, because their family labor supplies appear to be larger than the labor demands of their farm systems. Structural change thus could affect a great many farm systems in these four provinces of southern Italy - as many as 90 percent of the farms and 80 percent of the area (Table 4.12).

Conclusion

This part of southern Italian agriculture has a small farm sector that appears well-integrated in the greater economy and largely competitive with the rest of the agricultural sector and the regional economy. Most of the farm systems and a substantial majority of small farms and cultivated area are competitive. Small farms show much dependence on CAP policies after MacSharry reforms, but unless subsidies are lowered below their long-run expected levels, small farms will offer competitive returns. Feasible adjustments by the sector in response to the MacSharry changes increase the extent of competitiveness only modestly. Reductions in livestock, particularly beef and dairy animals, seem particularly likely in the post-MacSharry environment, and farmers face incentives to expand or introduce specialty crops.

Table 4.10
Employment effects of Southern Italy* farming systems

Total employment (≥ 1 FTE)	No of Systems				% No of Farms				% Arable Land			
	Val-d'Agri	Ufita-Alta Irpinia	Basso Molise-Alta-Capitanata	Total	Val-d'Agri	Ufita-Alta Irpinia	Basso Molise-Alta-Capitanata	Total	Val-d'Agri	Ufita-Alta Irpinia	Basso Molise-Alta-Capitanata	Total
Autonomous	6	2	3	11	11.7	2.0	23.8	37.5	15.5	2.2	45.4	63.1
Potentially autonomous	1	3	3	7	6.7	23.4	10.5	30.6	4.8	7.2	9.0	21.0
Non-autonomous	-	1	2	3	-	2.3	29.6	31.9	-	1.2	14.7	15.9
TOTALS	7	6	8	21	18.4	17.7	63.9	100.0	20.3	10.6	69.1	100.0

Classification of Southern Italy farming systems according to their capacity to absorb family labor surplus

Available labor	Val-d'Agri	Ufita-Alta Irpinia	Basso Molise-Alta-Capitanata	Total	Val-d'Agri	Ufita-Alta Irpinia	Basso Molise-Alta-Capitanata	Total	Val-d'Agri	Ufita-Alta Irpinia	Basso Molise-Alta-Capitanata	Total
Capacity to absorb	1	1	1	3	1.5	0.7	5.7	7.9	1.4	1.4	19.1	21.9
Potential capacity to absorb	3	3	2	8	11.4	11.6	21.7	44.7	13.9	5.7	30.5	50.1
No capacity to absorb	3	2	5	10	5.5	5.4	36.5	47.4	5.0	3.5	19.5	28.0
TOTALS	7	6	8	21	18.4	17.7	63.9	100.0	20.3	10.6	69.1	100.0

Source: Team estimates

*Southern Italy here refers only to provinces of Avellino, Potenza, Foggia and Campobasso

Table 4.11
Southern Italy* farming systems, long run viability

Types of systems	No of Systems				% No of Farms				% Arable Land			
	Val-d'Agri	Ufita-Alta Irpinia	Basso Molise-Alta-Capitanata	Total	Val-d'Agri	Ufita-Alta Irpinia	Basso Molise-Alta-Capitanata	Total	Val-d'Agri	Ufita-Alta Irpinia	Basso Molise-Alta-Capitanata	Total
Viable and competitive	1	1	1	3	1.5	0.7	5.7	7.9	1.4	1.4	19.1	21.9
Viable but potentially competitive	3	3	2	8	11.4	11.6	21.7	44.7	13.9	5.7	30.5	50.1
Potentially viable but competitive	2	-	3	5	2.1	-	6.9	9.0	1.8	-	4.8	6.6
Potentially viable and potentially competitive	1	1	-	2	3.4	3.1	-	6.5	3.2	2.3	-	5.5
Non-competitive	-	1	2	3	-	2.3	29.6	31.9	-	1.2	14.7	15.9
TOTAL	7	6	8	21	18.4	17.7	63.9	100.0	20.3	10.6	69.1	100.0
With neutral structural impact	1	-	1	2	0.5	-	5.7	6.2	2.9	-	19.1	22.0
With a necessary structural impact	3	2	5	10	5.5	5.4	36.5	47.4	5.0	3.5	19.5	28.0
With a potential structural impact	3	4	2	9	12.4	12.3	21.7	46.4	12.4	7.1	30.5	50.0
TOTAL	7	6	8	21	18.4	17.7	63.9	100.0	20.3	10.6	69.1	100.0

Source: Team estimates

*Southern Italy here refers only to provinces of Avellino, Potenza, Foggia and Campobasso

93

Table 4.12
Relative importance of different adjustments, by zones

Types of adjustment	Val-d'Agri		Ufita-Alta Irpinia		Basso Molise-Alta-Capitanata	
Crop mix and/or technological changes	67.5	73.6	68.2	62.0	37.4	61.0
Farm size and/or off-farm employment increases	12.4	9.5	-	-	11.7	9.6
Both types of adjustments	20.1	16.9	18.2	25.0	-	-
Off-farm employment or other income source	-	-	13.6	13.0	50.9	29.4
TOTALS	100.0	100.0	100.0	100.0	100.0	100.0

Source: Team estimates

The forgoing generalizations are not meant to imply that small farm agriculture is without structural problems. For as much as one-third of the farming population in the study area (and a smaller proportion of the cultivated area) there is little prospect of receiving competitive rates of return to domestic factors, even with major changes in the farm systems. For this group, access to other employment and outmigration from the sector offer the best hope of economic improvement.

Off-farm employment opportunity also is important to many small farms that offer competitive rates of return. Many farm families have more labor available for work than a small farm can absorb. Most small farms provide full employment for one family member, but available workers usually exceed this amount. Factor market legislation, that allows labor free access to work opportunity, and industrial development policy, that influences the location and accessibility of employment opportunity, thus will have a major impact on the future success of small farm agriculture.

5 Small farms in Central Italy

Gabriele Dono, Simone Severini and Alessandro Sorrentino

The hilly rainfed areas of Mediterranean Italy are among the most sensitive to CAP reform because these areas specialize in cereal and livestock production. The region selected for investigation, the Viterbo-Grosseto area in Lazio and Tuscany, is typical of much of central Italian agriculture. It is a dry hilly environment, with a small share of the labor force engaged in agriculture and relatively good opportunities for off-farm employment. The opportunity costs of labor resources are high and the pressures on small farm agriculture are great. The survival of small farms depends not only on the potentials to offer farmers relatively high rates of return to resources, but also to offer employments that can be integrated easily into a pluri-employment strategy that includes the non-agricultural sectors (Saraceno, 1994). Together with agro-ecological conditions, this requirement puts constraints on the types of farm systems that small farmers can consider. Systems like dairy or beef thus face pressures not only from new CAP policies, but also from the timing and incidence of labor input requirements (Gasson, 1988). Such systems are difficult or impossible to operate on a part-time basis. The niche for small farm agriculture is likely to include farm systems that are complementary to the requirements of off farm employment. Without such possibilities, agriculture will be left to larger, full-time farms.

Description of the study area

Dry hilly conditions typify nearly two-thirds of the agricultural area of Tuscany and Lazio. This environment is even more prominent in the study areas of Grosseto and Viterbo, comprising 81 and 87 percent of their agricultural areas, respectively. Most of the land area of Grosseto and Viterbo is in agro-forestry activity (83 and 75 percent, respectively), most people live in towns with less than 50,000 inhabitants, and population densities are relatively low. Even so, agriculture makes a relatively minor contribution to the regional economies. By 1990, agriculture accounted for only 9 and 7 percent of value added in Grosseto and Viterbo, respectively. This share has declined steadily in recent years, and the service sector has taken a dominant role. Income levels in Grosseto and Viterbo are relatively low; per capita incomes in the two areas are only about 85 percent of the regional average.

With the exception of a few areas suited to hazelnut and horticultural production, agriculture in the two areas is dominated by annual crops and pastures (Map 5.1). Excluding hazelnut areas, about 70 percent of the agricultural area is planted to crops, particularly cereals and forages. About 15 percent of the area is in pastures. This pattern results in much animal production, particularly sheep and dairy cows. Sheep represent more than half the value of the animal stock. Cows account for between 30 and 40 percent of the value and are especially important in Viterbo. Only about 10 percent of the area is irrigable; most of the irrigated perimeters are located in the coastal plains and produce horticulture for the Rome market. Shortages of irrigation limit greatly the potential to increase fruit or horticultural production. Even the introduction of yield increasing technology in forages and cereals are limited by the lack of water resources.

Principal differences between the agriculture in Grosseto and Viterbo reflect farm structure, attributed primarily to the effects of the Agrarian Reform of the 1950s. With the objective of consolidating medium size farms, the reforms much affected Grosseto but were largely ignored in the hilly parts of Viterbo. Grosseto farms average 2 parcels, each about 6 ha in size. Viterbo farms average 2.3 parcels, with an average parcel size of about 2.5 ha. Land is less equally distributed in Grosseto. There, 30 percent of the farms (in the 10-50 ha size class) cultivate 50 percent of the land. In Viterbo, 36 percent of the farms (in the 2-20 ha size class) cultivate 40 percent of the land.

Average farm size in Grosseto is 12.5 ha, whereas that in Viterbo is 5.5 ha. Grosseto farms provide more employment; estimates for Grosseto and Viterbo are 200 and 100 days of work per year, respectively. Although the Grosseto systems are larger, Viterbo farms offer higher intensities of labor use. Overall, however, agricultural employment patterns are dominated by the totals per farm. About 71 percent of the Grosseto farm families have no off-farm employment; the corresponding figure for Viterbo is 58 percent. Off farm employment is rather evenly distributed in Viterbo among the public sector, services, industry, and commerce sectors Commerce and hotel services are the most important sectors in Grosseto; the latter opportunities are indicative of the importance of tourism in the area.

Farm families are much smaller than in earlier years. About 45 percent of the families in each of the regions contain only 2 members; most of these households are comprised of old people. Another 45-50 percent of the families in the two regions contain 3 or 4 members. Rural families larger than 4 members are very rare.

Map 5.1 Study areas in Central Italy

The representative farm systems

Work to identify the relevant farm systems began with examination of FADN (Farm Accounting Data Network) data for the period 1989-91. Analysis of preliminary Census data allowed categorization of FADN farms. Cropping patterns are shown in Table 5.1, grouped by the FADN farm system (OTE) classification. In two of the groups, a single output dominates - hazelnuts in cluster 2, and horticulture in cluster 7. Areas emphasizing hazelnuts or horticultural crops were discarded from the study typology to allow a focus on the dry hilly areas. Clusters 3 and 5, specializing in olives, represent only a few communi in the area and representative farms for these groups were not developed.

Attention thus focused on farm types 1, 4, and 6. Type 1 represents nearly half the agricultural income of the study area. Its production pattern emphasizes cereals, forages, pastures, and sheep. Farm groups 4 and 6 account for another 25 percent of the region's income and represent a similar production pattern among cereals, forages, and animal production.

A questionnaire, developed to collect information about labor availability, farm structure, and production patterns, was distributed to 46 of the FADN farms. This survey was supplemented by an additional survey of 150 farms to obtain further information about demographic characteristics, production patterns, and technologies.

Analysis of the FADN data allowed construction of a typology of representative farms. The construction of representative farm models involved more work than just averaging the results of farm survey data. Such approaches could generate incongruous combinations of technical and managerial characteristics or structure and farm resource endowments. Although averages gave useful starting points in the characterization of a representative farm system, careful inspection of the resulting model was necessary to ensure consistency of the various characteristics. If necessary, values of particular variables were adjusted to ensure correspondence between farming practices and resource endowments. The opinions of expert observers and information gathered during fieldwork was critical in establishing 'sensible' and consistent farm models. The results of this analysis also were compared to the Census data to ensure that the representative farms were typical of the farms in the area. In total, ten systems were defined to represent the small and medium-sized farms of Viterbo and Grosseto (Table 5.2). The systems can be grouped in four categories of farms - crop, dairy, sheep, and mixed crop and livestock farms.

The crop oriented farms (VA1 and GA1), 13 and 18 ha, are typical of most of the cultivated area in Viterbo and Grosseto. Land quality is reasonable, and slopes are moderate. The parcels are not irrigable. Cropping patterns emphasize winter cereals (durum wheat) and forages. Oilseeds were not included in the Viterbo system; these are found only on farms with irrigation. Sunflower is included in the Grosseto system, where soil quality allows some rainfed production. The farms are relatively well equipped with machinery. Each farm has two tractors and implements. Most of the stock appears under-utilized, which contributes to a long working life and a relatively aged stock.

Table 5.1
Crop patterns of farms in Viterbo and Grosseto, 1990

Commodity

Crop System (OTE)	Cereals	Horti-culture	Forages-Pastures	Other Crops	Olive	Vine-yards	Fruits	Cows	Sheep	Other Animals	TOTAL
					(percent of gross margins)						
1. Cereals-Forages-Sheep	21.4	4.0	21.8	9.9	7.8	7.3	3.7	7.9	13.6	2.5	100
2. Hazelnuts	3.1	0.4	3.3	0.6	3.8	4.4	79.4	3.1	1.3	0.4	100
3. Olive-Vineyard	0.0	0.0	0.0	0.6	20.6	71.9	5.8	0.0	0.0	1.2	100
4. Mixed Crops	14.8	8.2	12.4	7.5	14.8	7.1	21.4	4.2	6.3	3.2	100
5. Olive	11.9	0.4	11.6	0.4	48.0	5.2	14.7	3.0	3.4	1.5	100
6. Cer-Forg-Oth.Crops-Sheep	27.6	8.7	12.5	20.0	4.0	7.3	3.2	6.3	7.1	3.4	100
7. Horticulture-Cereals	26.6	31.7	12.4	8.0	1.9	4.7	3.4	3.3	6.8	3.1	100

Source: FADN survey

Table 5.2
Characteristics representative farms, Viterbo and Grosseto

		Crop Oriented		Dairy			Sheep (Milk Production)				Mixed
		Viterbo	Grosseto	Viterbo Dairy	Viterbo Dairy-beef	Grosseto Dairy-Beef	Viterbo	Viterbo	Grosseto	Grosseto	Grosseto
		VA1	GA1	VB1	VB2	GB1	VO1	VO2	GO1	GO2	GM1
Land:											
Total Cultivated Land	(Ha)	13.1	18.2	15.3	12.7	18.8	49.9	76.0	28.3	60.7	16.9
Rented Land	(Ha)	0.0	0.0	3.8	0.0	3.4	33.4	54.0	3.7	11.2	2.6
Irrigated Land	(Ha)	0.0	0.0	5.4	0.0	0.7	0.0	0.0	0.0	0.0	0.0
Number of Parcels	(N)	4	6	3	5	7	6	5	7	12	7
Average Parcel Size	(Ha)	3.3	3.0	5.1	2.5	2.7	8.3	15.2	4.0	5.1	2.4
Crops:											
Cereals(ha)		8.5	8.7	2.3	3.6	8.1	15.7	11.0	6.5	18.3	7.7
Fodder Crops(ha)		3.1	4.0	13.0	7.6	9.4	33.0	65.0	20.0	40.6	8.5
Livestock:											
Herd Size (Bovine Equiv.)[a]	(N)	0.0	0.0	29.2	18.0	19.5	28.0	60.0	16.0	29.0	6.0
Labor:											
Total Used Labor Units	(FTE)	0.40	0.83	1.51	1.44	1.52	1.74	2.51	1.37	1.88	0.62
Total Available Labor Units[b]	(FTE)	1.45	1.60	1.72	1.74	1.91	2.23	3.73	1.95	2.89	1.72
Used LU/Available LU	(%)	27.9	51.7	87.7	82.3	79.6	78.2	67.3	70.2	65.1	35.9
Family Structure:											
Farmer Age Age	(Years)	50	56	47	53	50	49	49	42	45	55
Active Family Members[c] AFM	(N)	3	4	3	3	3	3	4	2	3	3
AFMs working off-farm[d] AFMoff	(N)	1	2	1	1	1	0	0	0	0	1
Off-farm/Total Active	(%)	33.3	50.0	33.3	33.3	33.3	0.0	0.0	0.0	0.0	33.3
Machinery:											
Number of Tractors	(N)	2	2	2	2	2	2	1	3	3	2
HP per Unit of Land	(HP/Ha)	9.3	6.3	8.1	7.5	7.7	3.3	1.0	7.1	3.1	6.9

Notes: a. 1 Bovine equivalent=10 sheep
    b. Total Available Labor Units   All members living on farm.
    c. Active Family Members   All members working on or off farm. Students and retired people are not included.
    d. AFMs working off-farm   All members working off farm.

Source: Team survey

Total labor use is only a third to a half of the time available. This is partly because of the marked seasonality in labor demands, that peaks for the harvest of wine grapes and olives. Typically, grown children live on the farm, but they work full time in off farm jobs.

The dairy-beef systems (VB1, VB2, GB1) produce milk. The VB1 farm is completely specialized in milk. In the other systems, meat represents about 25 percent of the value of output. The farms are relatively small, ranging in size from 13 to 19 ha. However, managerial ability and land quality is much better in the VB1 farm. About one-third of the land is irrigable with the result that forage production and animal carrying capacity is higher than in the other systems. Forage crops account for more than half of the cultivated area on all the systems. Small areas are planted to olives and vineyards. In the Grosseto system, some area is planted also to durum wheat. VB1 has 24 cows, whereas the other systems have only half as many animals. The groups differ also in capital stock. The VB1 system has larger and newer machinery, a completely mechanized operation for hay harvesting and storage, and modern barns and milking facilities. Family structure is similar to that of the crop oriented farms. Family labor is nearly fully utilized in these systems, reflecting the constancy of labor demands. The labor requirements of VB1 are relatively less than those of the other systems because of the greater extent of mechanization.

The sheep systems (VO1, VO2, GO1, GO2) emphasize milk production for cheese, using the Sarda breed. Farms range from 28 to 76 ha in size, carrying between 160 and 600 adult females (10 sheep=1 bovine equivalent). Viterbo farm systems are relatively fragmented; these farms typically rent in substantial amounts of land, often 4 or more km from the farm center. This pattern of land use requires substantial migration of the herd during production and proves a potentially important constraint to the introductions of improved infrastructure and sanitary controls. Land is not irrigable, which limits the potential to introduce higher yielding forages, such as alfalfa. Forages are planted each year; some coarse grains, such as barley and oats, are planted in winter. The Viterbo systems have less capital stock than the Grosseto systems. For example, Viterbo systems rely on hand milking and lack milk parlors and refrigeration. Machinery for crops is also less extensive, because Viterbo farms rely more on pasture and limit hay production.

Sheep systems require all available family members; full time off farm work is rare, and sons typically join the farm activity after graduation from high school. Labor demands show some seasonality, reaching a peak in the spring, when milk production reaches a peak and hay is harvested. The families of the largest farms, such as the Viterbo systems, usually do not live on the farm.

The mixed farm system (GM1) is diversified between crop production and sheep for milking. Farm size is 17 ha. Almost all land is devoted to forages and winter cereals, such as durum wheat and oats. A small area of vineyard and olives is maintained for home consumption. Herd size is 60 adult females. Milking is mechanized, but the parlor is small and the operation is time consuming. Family structure is similar to that of the other farm systems. The farmer's children work full time off the farm. Sons and the wife help with farm activities during the peak season demands.

Determination of the prominence of each of the systems within the local agriculture was based on linkages between the farm models and the ISTAT typologies (Table 5.3) used in the 1990 Census of Agriculture. The ISTAT typology defines farms in term of their technical and economic orientation (OTE). Comparison with the Census data showed that the representative farms for Viterbo and Grosseto capture the major variations of farm systems in the area. The farm types considered by the representative farm models represent 64 and 41 percent, respectively, of the area and the number of farms in the areas. The relevance to CAP reform is even larger than these numbers indicate, since the research purposely excluded commodities outside the reform process. The irrigation perimeters, concerned primarily or exclusively with fruit and vegetable production, were not considered. When these typologies are excluded from the farm census, the representativeness of the farm models in Viterbo and Grosseto increases to 70 percent of the cultivated area and 51 percent of the farms..

This comparison to the Census data presumes that economies of size within each farm type can be ignored, a reasonable presumption given the inclusion in the farm models of different farm sizes for similar commodity mixes (sheep farms, for example, are as large as 76 ha). The presence of a substantial rental market in machinery services probably contributes also to the absence of substantial disadvantages to small farm size. Dairies for cow milk are the most prominent exception to the above characterization. The largest dairy operations are large farms and have very different characteristics from the farms considered here. Still, average farm sizes for dairies in the two areas are only 16 ha, approximately the same as the sizes of the representative dairy farms. The representative farm models are thus typical for the region and for small farm agriculture.

Baseline economic results

A farm system is judged competitive if the returns to labor equal or exceed the returns to labor in non-farm employment. Off farm job opportunities are ample, and farmers can readily compare the rewards to farm work with wages in non-agricultural pursuits. The average off farm wage in the Viterbo-Grosseto area was 16.2 million lira per year in 1991-92, or about 65,000 lira per 8 hour day ($US 43). Competitiveness is evaluated with and without subsidies to determine the necessity of CAP supports. Another set of evaluations, termed viability, is made to determine the ability of the system to retain resources in the short-run. This calculation assumes that all owned capital and owned land are sunk costs and computes the returns to all owned resources per unit of family labor. This calculation shows the capacity of the system to cover variable costs in the short run.

The returns to labor in each of the farm systems are presented in Table 5.4. The results show a clear advantage for the largest dairy system and sheep systems in Viterbo. There, net returns to labor are a third larger than the market

Table 5.3
Representativeness of farming systems

	Total Province		Study Area*	
	N.Farms	Land	N.Farms	Land
		(percent)		
Viterbo				
VA1	30.9	51.8	42.1	59.4
VB1	0.8	2.0	1.1	2.3
VB2	0.5	2.4	0.7	2.7
VO1	5.7	7.3	7.8	8.4
VO2	0.2	3.7	0.3	4.2
Total	38.1	67.2	52.0	77.0
Grosseto				
GA1	35.8	45.1	39.1	46.6
GB1	1.3	2.9	1.4	3.0
GO1	1.9	6.2	2.1	6.4
GO2	0.2	1.6	0.2	1.7
GM1	7.0	5.8	7.6	6.0
Total	46.2	61.6	50.4	63.7
Viterbo+Grosseto	**40.6**	**64.4**	**51.3**	**70.1**

*Excluding horticulture and tree crops.
Source: Team survey, Census data

Table 5.4
Economic results for Viterbo-Grossetto systems, 1991-92

System	Size(ha)	Revenues	Costs Intermediate Inputs	Capital	Other Costs	Land	Hired Labor	Labor Returns Total	Labor Returns Returns/day	Total without subsidies	Viability Total	Viability Returns/day
						('000 1991 Lira)						
VA1	13.10	27630	10525	6412	1626	4585	0	4483	42.6	1378	14579	138.4
GA1	18.30	45064	11961	8721	2304	6405	0	15673	72.4	11621	30799	142.3
VB1	15.30	93418	28075	15674	8151	5355	0	36163	91.8	37049	57321	145.6
VB2	12.70	49641	16987	8401	4534	4445	0	15274	40.7	14636	29001	77.3
GB1	18.80	63261	22689	13881	5117	6580	0	14994	37.8	13406	35147	88.6
VO1	49.90	102471	26511	13376	5543	17465	0	39576	86.9	30681	60142	132.0
VO2	76.00	183001	55437	15008	10533	26600	4926	70497	99.4	55389	95355	134.4
GO1	28.30	66149	16366	12574	6114	9904	0	21191	59.2	15141	43866	122.5
GO2	60.70	119758	36558	16659	10992	21245	177	34127	69.4	22699	71005	144.5
GM1	16.90	32386	9166	8854	3905	5915	0	4546	28.2	851	19501	121.1

Source: Team estimate

wage rate. The sheep and crop systems for Grosseto also offer returns that are competitive with those earned in the non-agricultural sector. One reason that these systems are not more widespread is suggested by the cost data - cash flow constraints. These systems have the highest financial costs of the ten systems, often two or three times as much as those of the less profitable systems. The lowest rates of return are for the crop system in Viterbo, the diversified dairy and beef systems, and the diversified crop and sheep system in Grosseto. Returns to labor in these systems are sometimes less than half of the off farm wage rate. These systems also have the lowest requirements for purchased inputs.

Returns to the unprofitable systems would be even lower, often much lower, without EC subsidies (Table 5.4). The least profitable systems exist partly because of subsidy programs but also because of special circumstances for some farm families, such as limited access to the off farm labor market (the systems with beef and dairy production use more labor per farm, albeit at a low rate of return), limited availability of farm labor on some farms (the crop-oriented systems are the most labor extensive of all the systems and thus most amenable to part-time farming), or the importance of the house and garden to the family. Although not competitive, these systems are viable in the short-run. Presuming fixed costs to be sunk, returns to family labor often are double the level of off farm wages But without further changes in economic incentives, these systems would be expected to disappear gradually from the agricultural sector as capital stocks are fully depreciated and opportunities arise to sell land.

The most profitable systems in the region are the four relatively large sheep systems and the specialized dairy of Viterbo. Most of these systems are competitive even without EC subsidies. Specialization in milk production, whether from cows or sheep, is by far the most efficient (and input intensive) use of agricultural resources. The dairy system is relatively modern and has a much larger carrying capacity than the dairy-beef systems. This system also is very demanding of managerial talent to maintain milk quality as quantity is increased. The sheep systems take advantage of the region's natural pastures and use a highly productive and well-adapted breed. Among the sheep farms, economies of scale are present; differences between Viterbo and Grosseto arise because the Viterbo farms place greater reliance on pastures and have less capital-intensive (and less costly) milking techniques. The most profitable systems offer more than one FTE (2000 hours) of employment, contributing further to their solid footing as competitive farm systems.

Table 5.5 summarizes the baseline results in terms of farm numbers and cultivated area. The population of farms in the survey is used as the basis for the calculations. Although the farm sample does not provide universal coverage of all farms, most of the region's agriculture and the small farm systems that will be much affected by the CAP reform are included. In the baseline year, all farms are viable, but only about one half are competitive. When land area is considered, the share of competitive farms is about the same (nearly half). The non-competitive systems - crop farms in Viterbo, mixed crop and animal farms, and mixed dairy and beef systems - account for half of cultivated area and farms. Rates of return to labor in the hilly areas thus are adequate to retain resources in production in the short-run. But even without

Table 5.5
Competitiveness of the hilly regions of Italy, 1992

Type of Systems	No of systems			% of No of farms			% of arable land		
	VIT	GRO	Total	VIT	GRO	Total	VIT	GRO	Total
Competitive w/out direct support	3	0	3	12.0	0.0	20.2	9.7	0.0	9.7
Competitive with direct support	0	2	2	0.0	24.9	31.4	0.0	37.7	37.7
Non-competitive but viable in the short run	2	3	5	56.1	7.0	48.4	40.5	12.1	52.6
Noncompetitive and non-viable	0	0	0	0.0	0.0	0.0	0.0	0.0	0.0
TOTAL	5	5	10	68.1	31.9	100.0	50.2	49.8	100.0

Source: Team estimates

changes in economic incentives from CAP reforms, many farms will be pressured to change over the long run, either exiting the sector or becoming increasingly specialized in particular commodities. Structural change of agriculture remains a substantial economic phenomenon

Future competitiveness of the representative farming systems

The economic situation of hilly agriculture in the early 1990s was relatively good. Many of the farm systems were competitive, particularly sheep and milk systems. But the incentive structure for almost all of these systems will change radically after the full implementation of CAP reforms. Prices will decline for most of the important commodities, such as durum wheat and milk. Further, the introduction of quantitative controls and sanitary regulations will alter the production environment.

The effects of the MacSharry reforms

The expected prices for inputs and outputs after CAP reform are applied to the baseline results to generate a "post-MacSharry baseline" (Table 5.6). These results show the net returns to farm systems if farmers continue their previous production practices. Net revenues of most of the farm systems in Viterbo and Grosseto decline by 8 or 9 percent. Declines are greatest for the dairy-beef systems and the mixed crop and animal system in Grosseto (20 to 28 percent). The immediate impact of MacSharry reform thus is to worsen the economic situation of farms, especially for the poorest farms. Five of the systems remain competitive. All of the systems maintain short-run viability, although the dairy-beef systems barely succeed in doing so.

Almost all commodity prices decline on the crop oriented farms, especially for durum wheat (-42 percent) and oilseeds (-45 percent). The impact of price reductions is partially offset by direct subsidies, which increase from 9-12 percent of revenues to about 20-25 percent after the MacSharry reforms. But such payments are not sufficient to offset a decline in the net return to labor. The largest decreases are experienced in the dairy-beef systems; these systems fare poorly under CAP reform because meat revenues decline sharply, by more than 40 percent. Milk revenues decline only 8 percent, and the dairy and sheep systems show relatively less deterioration in returns to labor. Subsidy payments per sheep (up to 500 head) help the revenue position. Costs decline sharply in many of these systems, especially because of declines in feed costs. Still, labor returns fall.

In comparison to the 1991 results, the number of competitive systems declines only by one (from six to five), as the smallest sheep system returns fall to Lira 54,000 per day. Grosseto's crop-oriented farm barely remains competitive, and the specialized dairy and three of the sheep systems remain competitive. The biggest change after the MacSharry reforms is that all systems are now very dependent on direct subsidies. Without subsidies, only the dairy system is competitive, and the rest offer returns that are half or less of

Table 5.6

Summary of baseline results, Post-MacSharry

Viterbo and Grosseto

| System | Returns to Utilized Labor ('ooo of 1991 Lira/day) | | |
| | Competitiveness | | Viability |
	Without Subsidies	With Subsidies	
VA1	-33.8	39.9	143.2
GA1	23.3	66.1	135.8
VB1	83.9	83.9	135.6
VB2	28.9	32.6	68.1
GB1	20.1	30.1	79.6
VO1	51.2	80.3	124.7
VO2	58.2	91.3	126.9
GO1	28.6	53.7	112.2
GO2	23.4	63.1	137.6
GM1	-20.7	19.9	104.5

Source: Team estimates

the off-farm wage rate. Without subsidies, hilly region agriculture would suffer intense pressures for change and adjustment.

Possible changes in crop mix and technologies

Farmers will not ignore the deterioration in returns to farming activities from CAP reform. Changes are dramatic for almost all of the farm systems; even those systems that continue to offer returns greater than the off-farm wage rate suffer substantial deterioration in returns. All farmers face the prospect of markedly lower incomes. Whereas the incentive for change is great, a number of important constraints limit the potential for farms to alter dramatically their production patterns and technologies. The hilly terrain and lack of irrigation potential limit the crop alternatives; in particular, the production of commodities that are outside CAP regulations is difficult.

Institutional arrangements are important potential constraints as well. Quota systems are introduced for durum wheat, milk, and sheep - the most important commodities of the region. Farmers wishing to specialize more in these commodities will need access to markets for quota rights, and without these, many avenues for change become impossible. This problem is particularly important in the milk market, because production in excess of the milk quota is subject to a super-levy (tax) that is close to the milk price. Farmers thus have no incentive to produce milk unless they have quotas. The quotas for wheat and sheep merely limit the amount of subsidy that can be paid. Farmers exceeding their quotas are not penalized; rather, they simply are excluded from subsidy payments on their surplus production.

Another key set of constraints involves the introduction of sanitary regulations concerning the production of dairy and sheep milk. The introduction and enforcement of legislation to ensure an hygienic standard will require that farms use particular technical devices and practices in the collection of milk. Legislation now specifies characteristics for barns, milking rooms, milking parlors, milk refrigerators, and sanitation practices. Most of these requirements can be met by devoting more time to cleaning, but others can be satisfied only by changes in infrastructure (floor and wall materials, windows, water distribution, and water quality), or building new infrastructure (separate rooms for sick animals, collection and treatment of organic matter, and the purchase of refrigeration equipment). Substantial changes will be needed to meet these requirements, particularly for small dairies and for sheep farms not accustomed to using a central milking parlor. Such facilities usually are absent on sheep farms with fragmented landholdings; institutional changes to allow increased activity in the land market may be essential to allow sheep producers to change sufficiently their production practices, especially in Viterbo.

The simulations considered here take account of both types of adjustments (Table 5.7). Changes in production practices are intended to be realistic alternative cropping patterns. Changes in technology or farm size may face capital investment constraints, but these are assumed to be overcome by access to credit or to rental markets for machinery and land. One constraint that is not ignored, however, concerns the land market and farm structure (Dono et al., 1995). Dramatic changes in legislation would be necessary to facilitate

Table 5.7
Summary of simulation results, Post-MacSharry

Viterbo and Grosseto

System	Returns to Utilized Labor ('ooo of 1991 Lira/day)		
	Competitiveness		Viability
	Without Subsidies	With Subsidies	
VA1	-88.6	61.4	174.5
GA1	21.3	73.7	140.0
VB1	80.9	80.9	134.4
VB2	37.6	39.9	84.1
GB1	27.3	36.7	98.3
VO1	34.4	62.7	113.0
VO2	79.9	118.4	175.6
GO1	27.6	52.7	115.9
GO2	22.0	61.7	137.1
GM1	38.4	54.2	112.9

Source: Team estimates

substantial change in the structure of sheep farms. The new sanitary regulations mean that such change may be essential to ensure the economic survival of these farm systems. But given the dramatic nature of reforms in the land market, the results here are made under the assumption of a fixed farm structure. The simulation results thus are useful to show the importance of land market reforms.

The most profitable set of changes in the crop oriented farm of Viterbo involves enlargement of the farm from 13 to 25 ha through increased land rental; this change allows the farm to spread fixed costs over a larger throughput. Labor requirements increase only about 10 percent relative to the base case and seem easily managed. The main change in cropping pattern has been to join the CAP general regime. The set-aside provision requires that 15 percent of the land be idled. Forage crops are eliminated in favor of rapeseed. The system becomes almost competitive, though not without the subsidy program; subsidies account for more than a third of revenues, and without them the system remains at the same (negative) level of profitability as in the post-MacSharry baseline.

The Grosseto system simulation (GA1) shows the effect of substituting sunflower for hay and cereals and joining the set-aside program. This farm is able to maintain the level of returns realized in 1991, but with a greater dependence on subsidies.

The dairy and dairy-beef simulations show the difficulties that will occur for meat producers and for dairy farmers conforming to the new sanitary regulations. For dairies that are relatively large and already specialized in milk production, accommodation to the new regulations requires only minimal adjustments; the main changes to representative farm VB1 involve introduction of facilities to collect and treat manure. Returns to labor decline only slightly relative to the post-MacSharry baseline and remain well above the opportunity cost of labor. Specialized dairies of two dozen cows (or larger) thus appear to have good potential to compete within the new CAP environment. Expansion of this system presumes that farmer ability can be improved as needed, to increase the number of farmers using the specialized dairy practices.

Results of simulations for the dairy-beef systems (VB2 and GB1) and the Grosseto mixed farm (GM1) are less encouraging. Substantial investments are needed to convert the dairy-beef systems into larger, more specialized dairies. Further, the scope for expansion is probably limited for most of these farms; the simulations report the results of adding two dairy cows, to attain a total herd of 14 animals. Returns increase somewhat relative to the post-MacSharry baseline, but remain well below the opportunity cost of labor - less than Lira 40,000 per day for the beef systems, and only Lira 54,000 for the crop and sheep farm. Unless the small dairy farm systems can double in size (and become like the Viterbo specialized dairy, with 24 cows), returns to dairy-beef farmers will not be adequate to encourage continuation of these activities. The results on the Grosseto mixed farm reflect a simulation of specialization in sheep milk production. A doubling of herd size, to 120 animals, increases returns to levels similar to those of the other small sheep systems in Grosseto, but remaining below the opportunity cost of labor.

Sheep farming returns are negatively affected by the sanitary regulations, to a greater degree than returns on the dairy farms. The fragmented structure of some sheep farms, such as the smaller Viterbo system (VO1), means that accommodation to the new regulations can be extremely costly. The simulation results for the smallest Viterbo system turn out worse than those for the post-MacSharry baseline. The Viterbo system relies on milking sheep in the field; the new regulations will require that the animals be taken to a central parlor for milking. This change, plus the addition of refrigeration and manure treatment, cause the new system to be much costlier than the present system, and returns drop by about 5 million lira per FTE (Lira 20,000 per day), below the opportunity cost of labor.

Similar levels of competitiveness are found in the small systems of Grosseto. Returns to the Grosseto systems are not much affected by the new regulations because these systems already use centralized milking parlors and refrigeration. Necessary accommodations to the new regulations involve mainly the construction of manure treatment systems, and these have only a small effect on the net returns to labor; the results in the simulations are nearly the same as those in the post-MacSharry baseline. However, returns are just below the competitive level, similar to those of the smaller Viterbo system and the simulation of the Grosseto mixed farm. All of the small systems remain viable, but replacement and renovation of capital stock seem unlikely without improvements in economic incentives.

Incentives are not a problem for the large sheep producers. In large systems, economies of scale appear important. Returns in the larger Viterbo system increase about 20 percent relative to the post-MacSharry baseline because the new milking technology allows for much more efficient use of labor. Total labor use declines by 25 percent in the larger system (with a 24-stall parlor), and this efficiency more than offsets the cost increases associated with the milking parlors. Time may be needed to adapt the herd to mechanical milking, but if these short-run complications can be managed, the resulting farm offers returns to labor that are well above the competitive level.

Implications for structural change

The hilly rainfed zones of Italian agriculture can expect dramatic changes in incentives as a result of CAP reform. The production of cereals, especially durum wheat, becomes less profitable, even with the set-aside and compensatory payment programs. Some substitution into oilseeds may help to maintain the competitiveness of crop farm systems, along with increased efficiency in the use of capital equipment. But the most prominent path to sustaining competitiveness involves increases in farm size. Only the largest farm systems offer competitive rates of return to farm labor, but some of the smaller systems are close.

The aggregate impact on the agricultural sector of changes in prices and the simulations of farmer response are summarized in Table 5.8. Under the projected price changes without adjustment, four of the systems remain competitive. Competitive farms account for about 52 percent of the population

114

Table 5.8
Hilly regions of Italy, projected competitiveness

Type of System	Projected prices without crop mix and/or technological changes			Projected prices with crop mix and/or technological changes		
	No of systems	% of No of farms	% of arable land	No of systems	% of No of farms	% of arable land
Competitive w/out direct support	2	1.8	4.1	2	1.8	4.1
Competitive with direct support	2	34.9	42.0	4	39.7	46.7
Non-competitive but viable in the short run	6	63.3	53.9	4	58.4	49.2
Noncompetitive and non-viable	0	0.0	0.0	0	0.0	0.0
TOTAL	10	100.0	100.0	10	100.0	100.0
Grosseto						
Competitive w/out direct support	0	0.0	0.0	0	0.0	0.0
Competitive with direct support	1	77.6	73.1	3	92.7	82.6
Non-competitive but viable in the short run	4	22.4	26.9	2	7.3	17.4
Noncompetitive and non-viable	0	0.0	0.0	0	0.0	0.0
TOTAL	5	100.0	100.0	5	100.0	100.0
Viterbo						
Competitive w/out direct support	2	2.7	8.2	2	2.7	8.2
Competitive with direct support	1	14.9	11.1	1	14.9	11.1
Non-competitive but viable in the short run	2	82.4	80.7	2	82.4	80.7
Noncompetitive and non-viable	0	0.0	0.0	0	0.0	0.0
TOTAL	5	100.0	100.0	5	100.0	100.0

Source: Team estimates

and 65 percent of the cultivated area. The simulations have relatively little impact on the results. Returns to farming can be increased in some of the systems, but not enough to change the categorization of many of them. The number of competitive farms increases to six (although three of the systems offer returns close to the off-farm wage), representing about 55 percent of the farms and 65 percent of the cultivated area.

CAP reform does not affect competitiveness very much, but it does alter the sources of competitiveness and the level of remuneration. Half of the systems in Viterbo and Grosseto offered competitive rates of return to labor in 1991. After CAP reform, returns in the previously unprofitable systems are less than the opportunity cost of labor and often below the rate of remuneration in 1991. Returns to five of the systems are lower in the post-MacSharry simulations (with farm adjustment to the new CAP) than in the 1991 base case. The outlook for the hilly rainfed areas under CAP reform thus appears bleak.

The only bright spots in this gloomy portrait of the agricultural sector involve the systems that are relatively specialized and large. The highest returns to labor occur in the dairy system, the specialized crops (especially the larger system of Grosseto), and the large sheep system. These systems provide returns that are competitive with those offered by the off farm sector; in the Viterbo sheep system, returns in post-MacSharry (with farmer adjustment) are even higher than they were in 1991. Of the commodities currently important in the area, only beef seems unable to remain as at least a part of a competitive system.

The importance of changes to larger farms is shown also by information about the labor demands of the farm systems (Table 5.9). Only 12 percent of the farms and 10 percent of cultivated area offer as much as one FTE of employment. Even with the simulated changes, most of the systems cannot increase to a level of autonomy. Provision of off farm employment or transformation of existing farm systems to imitate the larger systems thus are going to be important paths of change for the maintenance of a competitive agricultural sector.

These points are reiterated by the disaggregated results presented in Figure 5.1. The systems are classified in terms of competitiveness and degree of autonomy. The scatter of observations can be split into three groups. Farms in area A are competitive and have high levels of autonomy. These systems are specialized in sheep or dairy and most labor is provided by family members. Farms in area B are part time farms with an acceptable level of competitiveness but low levels of autonomy. These farms, among the most common in the study area, are oriented to crop production. Most family income comes from off farm employment and farm income is not large enough to sustain the family. Farms in area C have poor economic performance and require radical structural adjustment. In some cases, adjustment will free resources, while other cases require additional agricultural resources.

The arrows in Figure 5.1 show possible structural adjustment paths and the numbers along them indicate constraints to such strategies. These constraints make some adjustment patterns more likely than others and suggest policy actions that may be important to make them feasible. Movements within each area generally require limited structural adjustments. Usually they involve changes in crop mix, product specialization, and implementation of different

Table 5.9

Classification of farming systems according to their autonomy

Type of Systems	No of systems			% of No of farms			% of Arable land		
	VIT	GRO	Total	VIT	GRO	Total	VIT	GRO	Total
Autonomous (≥ 1 FTE)	3	0	3	17.6	0.0	12.1	19.3	0.0	9.6
Potentially autonomous	0	0	0	0.0	0.0	0.0	0.0	0.0	0.0
Non-Autonomous	2	5	7	82.4	100.0	87.9	80.7	100.0	90.4
TOTAL	5	5	10	100.0	100.0	100.0	100.0	100.0	100.0
Absorption of the family labor surplus									
Autonomous	2	0	2	2.7	0.0	1.9	8.2	0.0	4.1
Potentially autonomous	0	1	1	0.0	77.6	24.0	0.0	73.1	36.6
Non-Autonomous	3	4	7	97.3	22.4	74.1	91.8	26.9	59.3
TOTAL	5	5	10	100.0	100.0	100.0	100.0	100.0	100.0

Source: Team estimates

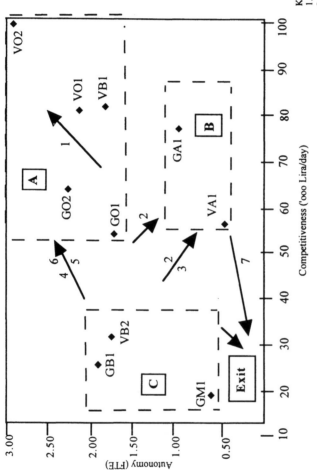

Key to constraints
1. Land and credit
2. Rights to durum wheat premiums
3. Demand for labor in the local market
4. Milk quotas
5. Land
6. Rights to sheep premiums
7. Demand of labor and land

Figure 5.1   Adjustment patterns for the representative systems

technologies. In general, these changes require limited farm investments. For example, the crop oriented farms (VA1 and GA1) improve economic performance by joining the general CAP regime, introducing the set aside, and increasing oilseed and olive production.

Adjustment across areas of the graph face more rigid constraints. These can be relaxed only by radical adjustment of the agricultural sector. Most of the pressure for structural adjustment comes from the unspecialized farms in area C. Simulations showed that their economic performance improves only slightly by increasing specialization. Their poor economic performances result from their small size - all these systems have small fodder production, constraining herd size. Dairy-beef farms (VB2 and GB1) cannot rely on irrigation to increase fodder availability and herd size. GM1 has little cultivated land. The new sanitary regulations only worsen economic performances.

Movements toward area A seem constrained by several factors. To increase herd size, beef and dairy farms need to increase on-farm feed production. This can be achieved by increasing their size (constrained by the limited mobility of land, constraint 5). This adjustment strategy also is constrained by the need to comply with sanitary regulations and to purchase new machinery. A further constraint results from EU quota policy. Dairy-beef farms can increase size only by purchasing additional milk quota (constraint 4). GM1 needs to purchase additional rights to enlarge the herd (constraint 6). The transition might not need extra financial resources if these farms had the opportunity to sell their durum wheat rights. However, this adjustment is constrained by land mobility as long as compensation is linked to land. Adjustment in the smaller sheep systems is difficult because of the sanitary regulations. These farms require radical change in structure and production techniques. In general, policies to increase land and quota mobility and access to credit increase the chances for livestock farms to move from area C to area A. Such interventions should increase the number of full time and specialized farms (Area A). Most of these movements presume also that managerial skills can increase as needed.

Easier adjustment strategies for farms in area C are to give up livestock farming and specialize in crop production, or to give up farming altogether. Part time crop farming can be a step towards exit from agriculture or a permanent transformation that provides an acceptable level of competitiveness. This adjustment strategy reduces labor use, meaning that off farm employment must increase. A dynamic local labor market (constraint 3) is required. In some cases, social security payments may substitute for lack of off farm labor opportunities. Also, crop oriented farms in this region are competitive only with the extra compensation for durum wheat (constraint 2). So long as durum wheat quotas are linked to land, farm changes require a well-developed land rental market. Availability of land with durum wheat quota will occur only if some farms give up farming

The extreme option available to all farming systems is to exit from agriculture. This shift depends on continued growth of the non-agricultural sectors. Exit is an option for uncompetitive farms that can not cope with structural constraints, and is necessary to make resources available for the structural adjustment of remaining farms. Increasing labor demand in the non-agricultural sectors can increase the rate of adjustment. However, the location of employment opportunities also plays an important role. If labor demand arises locally, a large number of farms in area B (part-time and crop oriented farms) probably will remain. However, if employment opportunities are located in other regions, more farms will leave. Exit will be reduced also by the growth in employment opportunities provided by the neighboring metropolitan area of Rome.

Table 5.10 shows the aggregate importance of changes in size and changes in crop mix or technologies as paths to a competitive agricultural sector. Crop mix and technology changes are sufficient to absorb family labor and retain a competitive rate of return to domestic resources only in Viterbo and there only for a small percentage of the systems. More important are changes in farm size or increases in off farm employment; these are sufficient changes for three-fourths of the Grosseto farms. Both types of change are important for about 15 percent of the Viterbo farms. For the other farm systems, the options for change involve leaving the sector to find off farm employment or transformation of their farm system into a system like one of the successful systems. Farms in this least successful category account for more than 75 percent of the farms in Viterbo and 22 percent of the farms in Grosseto.

Conclusion

The continuation of agriculture in the hilly regions seems assured for the next decade or two, if only because of asset fixity and the importance of sunk costs to the current population of farmers. But the future outlook for agriculture as a competitive sector is a different proposition. The sector has the potential to remain a competitive part of the economy, with rates of return to labor, capital, and land that are comparable to those offered elsewhere in the economy. Agriculture can be a thriving sector. But competitiveness will not be attained without substantial change. Farms, even small ones, need access to capital and land markets to realize the kinds of change modeled in this research. If factor markets are inaccessible, the progressive deterioration and abandonment of agricultural activity seems inevitable.

For a substantial share of the small farm agricultural population, exit from the sector seems the most likely option. Small, rainfed farms and small livestock operations do not presently offer much hope of returns that are competitive with off-farm opportunities. Without much irrigated area or with herd sizes too small to justify large-scale, fixed location milking parlors, farms have difficulty earning adequate rates of return to their labor and capital resources. These agro-environmental situations seem more successfully managed by 'full-time' operations. Such farms, primarily sheep, dairy, and cereal operations, may still be 'small' by EU economic standards, but they are large relative to historical traditions in the area, particularly in Viterbo. Some Viterbo farms also must overcome the limitations of a fragmented farm structure to accommodate better the new sanitary regulations.

Table 5.10

Relative importance of different adjustments, by zone

Type of Systems	VIT		GRO		TOTAL	
	% of No of farms	% of arable land	% of No of farms	% of arable land	% of No of farms	% of arable land
Crop mix and/or technological change	9.2	6.8	0.0	0.0	6.3	3.4
Farm size and/or off farm employment increases	0.0	0.0	77.6	73.1	24.8	36.4
Both types of adjustments	14.9	11.0	0.0	0.0	10.1	5.5
Off farm employment or other income sources	76.9	82.2	22.4	26.9	58.8	54.7
TOTAL	100.0	100.0	100.0	100.0	100.0	100.0

Source: Team estimates

121

Changes could occur to alter this pessimistic outlook. But they would have to be dramatic and far-reaching, including totally new production technologies, different crops, such as fruits that can tolerate rainfed conditions, and new post-farm systems to handle marketing and processing of products that at present are novel for these areas. Such developments undoubtedly would imply substantial new investments by the public sector in such areas as research and development. Regardless of which development path is followed, the agricultural structure for small farms in Central Italy will be much different from that at present.

6 The future for small farms in Southern Europe

Francisco Avillez, Eric Monke, Scott Pearson and Carlo Perone-Pacifico

Small farms in Portugal and Italy have strong similarities, sharing many characteristics of the agriculture of southern Europe. Farm families cultivate a diverse set of crops, and some attention is given to home consumption needs. Crops grown in the two countries are similar, with nearly universal presence of vineyards, cereals, and animals of one sort or another. Farms often are a multi-generational affair; grandparents and children are an integral part of the farm activity, participating in the conduct of required tasks. A strong ethic for land ownership has contributed to large numbers of small farms, a demand fueled in Portugal by the emergence of emigrant remittances and in Italy by sustained economic growth and the introduction of land reform programs. Rates of land turnover among small farmers are slow and prices seem surprisingly high. The intrinsic value of land has been reinforced further by the introduction of legislation to maintain small cultivator access and promote small farmer rights (Commission of the European Communities, 1982). Legislation is biased mostly in favor of small cultivators, even if policy implementation seems often preoccupied with larger producers.

But there also are important differences in the small farm sectors of the two countries. In the early 1990s, Portugal had a population of 10 million and a per capita income of $9,000; Italy had 57 million people and an income level per person of about $20,000. These differences are large, and they create major differences in the economic characteristics of small farm agriculture and the needs for policy support. The larger population size and higher income level of Italy means that local markets provide more scope for consumption of local production, particularly of specialty crops, and these crops occupy a special niche for small farmers. In Italy, crop production choices are more diverse and particular producers can specialize to a greater extent in the crops chosen.

These differences in economic status are associated with major contrasts in farm structure. Italian small farms are several times larger and usually much more consolidated than their Portuguese counterparts. Italian agriculture already has experienced substantial structural change, and small farms often are the consequence of economic growth rather than isolated from it. On-farm investments in infrastructure and land improvement mostly have been made. Portuguese farms, in contrast, are often too small and fragmented to offer acceptable returns to family labor, even with substantial changes in farm technologies and crops. For Portuguese small farm agriculture, much structural change has yet to take place, and many small farm families appear destined to leave agriculture in favor of other employment.

Much of the future for small farm agriculture depends on the conduct of policies, both agricultural and non-agricultural (Cioffi and Sorrentino, 1997). In agriculture, paramount importance attaches to the evolution of MacSharry policies, the innovation of new programs and supports, and the access provided to complementary inputs of land and capital. The introduction of MacSharry reforms came at an opportune time, when market prices for commodities were unusually high. Farmer reactions will be more strident if prices return to their long-run trends. The future conduct of EC compensatory payment programs has become increasingly important for small farm competitiveness. Substantial erosion in the level of compensatory payments will have dire consequences for small farmers' incomes.

The role of structural change policies and public investments to support agriculture differs between the countries. For Portugal, on-farm public investments have important effects on farm competitiveness. A large share of the small farm population is not competitive at present, but can become competitive with substantial improvements in infrastructure. In Italy, these interventions already have been done in large part. A sign of the superior state of public good provision is the larger degree of competitiveness of Italian small farm systems. Agronomic conditions much affect the potential for small farms. Rainfed cereal systems and animal production, for example, seem more amenable to full-time operations. But most other types of farm systems offer farmers competitive rates of return.

Further gains in incomes will depend increasingly on the development of new product markets and new institutions to facilitate small farmer access to markets, particularly for specialty crops. In adapting to new opportunities, farmer access to capital and land markets will have paramount importance. Such access does not require subsidies. More important than prices of the inputs is small farmer access to them. Small farmers may accept somewhat lower returns to their labor than market wages (Appendix, Chapter 2), and this phenomenon means that small farmers can potentially pay prices even higher than market prices for other inputs.

For non-agricultural policy, critical importance is attached to access to employment. Small farms often do not provide adequate employment opportunities relative to available family labor supplies. Nor are they competitive in all agro-ecological environments; for example, small farms have particular difficulties competing in rainfed areas producing cereals or in animal systems For various reasons, small farms are not going to solve Europe's employment problem. But in some areas, they can provide a substantial supplement to employment for a great many rural families. Access to non-agricultural employment depends on conditions of rural infrastructure, policies for rural development and rural industrialization, and regulations for rural labor markets.

Results

The two countries are at very different points in the structural adjustment process. Although there is no unique endpoint for the share of labor force engaged in agricultural employment, by 1990 Portugal's share (18 percent) was twice as large as Italy's (9 percent). The results of the farm surveys support the view that Portugal has much farther to go than Italy along the structural adjustment road. Portugal's small farms are smaller and more fragmented, and a larger proportion of farms have no identifiable prospects to gain competitive rates of return. This result is clear in the pre-MacSharry situation, and it remains equally clear after the MacSharry incentives are installed.

Portugal's agriculture has the opportunity to follow a similar path to that seen in Italy. Major improvements in Portuguese competitiveness would follow a concerted program of public and private investment in agriculture. This program would involve the sorts of investments - feeder roads, electrification, and small-scale irrigation - that have been done already in Italy. These investments, and the development path fostered by such investments, are well known to policy makers and development planners in Portugal.

A surprisingly large proportion of Italian small farms are competitive, particularly in the specialty crop areas. The smallest farm systems that produce the traditional CAP commodities - cereals, meat, and milk - fare less well than their larger, full-time counterparts But small farms do relatively well when irrigation is available and specialty crops can be produced. For Italy, the important new developments for small farms involve initiatives that are as yet unproved. Further adverse changes - more severe declines in agricultural incentives, or increases in the rate of return to off-farm employment - will heighten the pressure on small farms to change. The farming areas of central Italy are already experiencing these pressures. They have greater difficulty than farmers in the south in maintaining competitiveness in an economic environment of higher opportunity costs for labor and greater off farm opportunities. The agronomic environment appears also less amenable to small farm systems. The agricultural solutions to these problem situations in central Italy remain largely unknown, if they exist at all.

The farming systems

The study areas are distinctive in agro-climatic conditions and cropping patterns (Table 6.1). Rainfed annual crop systems were prominent in the selection of Italian zones because these systems are particularly vulnerable to the anticipated changes in the CAP. Irrigated systems are more common in the Portuguese sample, and the diversity in topography and crop orientation is larger. This difference reflects differences in the sample rather than incidence; Italy has many areas with irrigation that were excluded from this study.

Table 6.1

The Italian and Portuguese farming systems: agro-climatic zones and commodity orientation

Region and system	Southern Italy				Central Italy				Northern and Central Portugal			
	Selected Systems No	%	% No of Farms	% Arable Land	Selected Systems No	%	% No of Farms	% Arable Land	Selected Systems No	%	% No of Farms	%Arable Land
Plateau/Valley bottom	17	81.0	85.9	90.0	-	-	-	-	21	67.7	49.4	52.0
Rainfed Systems	(10)	47.6	49.7	45.8	-	-	-	-	(6)	19.4	16.7	16.2
Annual Crops	([3])	14.3	38.1	35.8	-	-	-	-	-	-	-	-
Permanent Crops	([2])	9.5	2.4	1.4	-	-	-	-	([5])	16.1	16.7	16.2
Livestock	([5])	23.8	9.2	8.6	-	-	-	-	([1])	3.2	-*	-*
Irrigated System	(7)	33.3	36.2	44.2	-	-	-	-	(15)	48.4	32.6	35.8
Annual Crops	([5])	23.8	33.9	42.5	-	-	-	-	([4])	12.9	1.3	5.5
Permanent Crops	([1])	4.8	1.7	1.4	-	-	-	-	([3])	9.7	0.7	2.4
Dairy	([1])	4.8	0.6	0.3	-	-	-	-	([8])	25.8	30.6	27.9
Hilly or Mountain Zones	4	19.6	14.1	10.0	10	100.0	100.0	100.0	10	32.3	50.6	48.0
Rainfed Systems	(4)	19.6	14.1	10.0	(9)	90	98.6	75.2	(10)	32.3	50.6	48.0
Annual Crops	([1])	4.8	9.0	3.4	([2])	20	79.9	-	-	-	-	-
Permanent Crops	-	-	-	-	-	-	-	-	([4])	12.9	32.8	26.9
Livestock	([3])	14.3	5.1	6.6	7	70	18.7	23.3	([6])	19.4	17.8	21.1
Irrigated Systems	-	-	-	-	1	10	1.4	1.5	-	-	-	-
Annual Crops	-	-	-	-	-	-	-	-	-	-	-	-
Permanent Crops	-	-	-	-	-	-	-	-	-	-	-	-
Dairy	-	-	-	-	1	10	1.4	1.5	-	-	-	-
TOTAL	21	100.0	100.0	100.0	10	100.0	100.0	100.0	31	100.0	100.0	100.0

Source: Team estimates

126

The zones include flat areas (plateaus or valley bottoms) and the hilly or mountainous zones. This categorization allows particular attention to the difference between irrigated and rainfed conditions, since irrigation usually is present only on flatlands. The prominence of the different topographies varies greatly by region. Most of the systems in southern Italy (17 of 21) are located in relatively flat areas. Seven of these systems are irrigated, emphasizing fruit, vegetables, and fodder crops. Mountainous and hilly conditions represent only 15 percent of farms and 10 percent of the cultivated area. Important commodities in these areas are tobacco, cereals, fodder crops, and sheep and goats. Most Italian systems in the hilly or mountainous areas (Viterbo, Grosseto, Val d'Agri, and Ufita-Alta Irpinia) are rainfed, representing more than 98 percent of farms and cultivated area. Annual crops are durum wheat, oilseeds, and forages. Livestock are important, emphasizing the production of dairy products, beef, and sheep. The livestock systems represent about 20 percent of farms and land area.

In northern and central Portugal, permanent crops play an important role and are prominent on half of the farms and 46 percent of the cultivated area. Next in importance are the animal production systems. Most systems (21 of 31) are located in flatlands and are irrigated. The predominant crops are maize and forages for dairy. Other important systems in the irrigated zones include fruit and vegetable farms. Rainfed systems in the flatlands emphasize vineyards and olives. Farm systems are more homogeneous in the hilly or mountainous zones; these zones also comprise a large part of the agricultural sector. The 10 systems in these zones account for half of farms and area. Permanent crops are important in these zones, as are beef and sheep production. Animal systems (6) account for about 20 percent of farms and cultivated area.

Farms in both countries are small by developed country standards, but Italian farms are much larger and more consolidated than Portuguese farms (Table 6.2). In southern Italy, more than 80 percent of farms and 70 percent of cultivated area are represented by farms between 5 and 20 ha in size; most are larger than 10 ha. Outside of the irrigated areas, farms are almost always larger than 10 ha. In the hilly regions, about three fourths of farms and 63 percent of the area is operated by farms between 10 and 20 ha. Farms in Portugal are smaller. Farms smaller than five ha account for three-fourths of farms and two-thirds of area. Most Portuguese farms are only a third or fourth as large as Italian farms. Portuguese farms also are much more fragmented, having two or three times as many parcels as Italian farms. Parcels in Italy thus are often five or six times as large as parcels in Portugal. This difference makes them more amenable to mechanization and also eases the burdens placed on agricultural infrastructure, particularly feeder roads.

Baseline economic results

The baseline results show the superior performance of Italian agriculture and suggest that Italian farms were better adjusted to economic circumstances of the early 1990s (Table 6.3). This pattern is consistent with the view that Portuguese agriculture has to undergo more structural adjustment. They reflect also the substantial changes brought to Portugal by accession to the

127

Table 6.2
The Italian and Portuguese farm systems, farm size

Farm size classes (ha)	Southern Italy				Central Italy				Northern and Central Portugal			
	Selected Systems		% No of Farms	% Arable Land	Selected Systems		%No of Farms	% Arable Land	Selected Systems		% No of Farms	% Arable Land
	No	No of parcels			No	No of parcels			No	No of parcels		
>5	1	4	9.0	3.4	-	-	-	-	11	10	78.0	66.7
5 - 10	6	2	38.1	23.4	-	-	-	-	9	14	3.7	9.6
10 - 20	10	3	44.5	48.4	6	5	87.9	85.5	7	9	17.3	17.3
20 - 40	2	4	2.2	2.8	1	7	1.3	5.0	2	11	0.4	3.1
>40	2	5	6.2	22.0	3	7	10.7	9.5	2	5	0.6	3.3
TOTAL	21	3	100.0	100.0	10	5	100.0	100.0	31	10	100.0	100.0

Source: Team estimates

128

Table 6.3
The Italian and Portuguese farming systems in the baseline year

Type of System	Southern Italy			Central Italy			Northern and Central Portugal			Total Systems
	No of systems	% of No of farms	% of arable land	No of systems	% of No of farms	% of arable land	No of systems	% of No of farms	% of arable land	
Competitive w/out direct support	14	54.2	75.5	3	12.0	9.7	12	3.4	10.5	29
Competitive with direct support	3	10.5	5.4	2	24.9	37.7	0	0.0	0.0	5
Non-competitive but viable in the short run	3	33.0	17.9	5	63.1	52.6	16	29.8	35.7	24
Noncompetitive and non-viable	1	2.3	1.2	0	0.0	0.0	3	66.8	53.8	4
TOTAL	21	100.0	100.0	10	100.0	100.0	31	100.0	100.0	62

Source: Team estimates

Community. Agricultural prices declined in real terms by about 50 percent between 1985 and 1992, largely as a consequence of harmonization with the CAP and EC prices and the substantial appreciation of the escudo. These adverse changes were not suffered by the Italian agricultural sector.

In Portugal, 12 of 31 systems were competitive, but these successful systems represented only 3 percent of farms and 10 percent of the cultivated area. The most profitable systems, located in the flatlands, had irrigation and produced maize and forages for dairy or fruits and vegetables. A few of the modernized vineyards were profitable as well. But these systems did not represent much of the small farm population. Only one-third of farms with 40 percent of area are competitive even in the short run (viable), where all fixed costs are considered sunk. This result reflects the prominence of labor intensive crops and production technologies. One reason that short-run viability measures are not so different from long-run competitiveness measures is that many systems do not have large capital and land costs to sink. Before CAP reform, most non-competitive farmers in Portugal could do better in off farm employment.

In Italy, more than two-thirds of the systems (22 of 31) offered returns equal or above market wages. In southern Italy, two-thirds of farms and 80 percent of cultivated area offered competitive returns. Farms producing irrigated fruits and vegetables do particularly well, but so do many of the rainfed systems raising animals, cereals, and tobacco. One region, Ufita-Alta Irpinia, fares worst. The hilly regions of central Italy also do not fare so well. Still, more than a third of farms and nearly half of the area was cultivated by competitive farm systems. Sheep production does particularly well, but competitive systems are found also in the other farm types, such as dairy and cereals. Many of these systems are large enough to be considered full-time operations, particularly when animals are involved. Almost all of the non-competitive Italian systems are viable in the short run. If fixed costs are considered sunk and all net returns are attributed to farm family labor, the implicit return to farm labor is higher than the off farm wage rate for almost all systems. This result reflects the prominence of non-labor factor costs, particularly capital, in the structure of total production costs.

Direct supports played relatively little role in the competitiveness of small farm agriculture (Table 6.3). Only 5 of the competitive systems owe their status to supports. More systems, such as dairy, received indirect subsidies through the system of institutional prices and were more dependent on market price supports than on direct support measures. The major exception to this tendency involved durum wheat in Italy, which was receiving area payments during the baseline year. Direct subsidies thus are most prominent in the rainfed zones of the Italian regions. Beef prices also were aided by EC programs, but these systems were not competitive. Many of the competitive systems benefited strongly from fruit and vegetable production, and these commodities were largely outside the CAP.

Impact of MacSharry reforms

The initial impact of the MacSharry reforms was estimated by modification of the baseline results. The "projected baseline" results show the impact on farm systems of changes in incentives without allowance for farm adjustment.

Output prices, input prices, and domestic factor prices were projected forward to the values expected to coincide with long-run market incentives. This was taken as the year 2000, and the changes were generally more draconian than the actual implementation of MacSharry. By the mid-1990s, strong international markets had prevented substantial price declines, and set aside criteria have been modest (for example, only five percent in 1997).

The projected prices reflect altered farm incentives (Table 6.4). The importance of direct support measures increases markedly. This effect is especially evident in the Italian systems (chosen partly for the prominence of CAP commodities). There the MacSharry reforms demonstrate the support of EU policy to agriculture. In southern Italy, the proportion of competitive farms dependent on direct supports increases from 10 to 30 percent and the share of cultivated area so dependent increases from 5 to 22 percent. In the hilly regions of central Italy, the number of farms dependent on subsidies increases from 25 to 35 percent and the dependent arable area increases slightly, from 38 to 42 percent. This shift reflects the effects of reforms in the cereals and livestock sectors, in which institutional prices are replaced by compensatory payments on land and animal herds.

Portuguese results are much less affected by the policy shift because the only important commodity to benefit from direct support measures is maize. Most farm systems that emphasize maize are not competitive, and the provision of supports is not sufficient to render the systems competitive. The direct income transfers associated with the less favored areas and the agro-environmental programs are similarly ineffective at increasing the competitiveness of Portuguese systems.

Another noticeable impact of the CAP reforms is the small impact on the competitiveness of Italian farming. In southern Italy, the number of competitive farms decreases only by about 5 percentage points and the competitive area decreases by less than 7 percentage points. In the central region, the decline in competitive systems is less than one percentage point for the number of farms and for arable area. Although the reforms alter income levels, they do not much affect competitive status. The level of compensation introduced by CAP reform almost offsets the negative effects of expected declines in intervention prices and the imposition of a set-aside. Also helpful to Italian agricultural profits is the projected depreciation of the Italian exchange rate to offset the appreciation during 1986-91.

In contrast, the projected price changes have a very positive impact on the Portuguese farming systems. The prominence of competitive systems increases from 3 to 18 percent of the population and from 10 to 22 percent of cultivated area. This result is not much related to the MacSharry reforms and instead reflects the improvement expected in horticultural and fruit prices, occasioned in turn by the expected depreciation of the escudo. Most improvements in profitability are captured by the systems outside of the CAP - the permanent crop and horticulture systems. The region most favored by the changes is the Oeste. Future expansion of these systems will require expansion of marketing systems and continued improvements in the quality of output.

Table 6.4
Italian and Portuguese projected competitiveness
(without crop mix or technological changes)

Type of Systems	Northern and Central Portugal		Southern Italy		Central Italy	
	% of No of farms	% of arable land	% of No of farms	% of arable land	% of No of farms	% of arable land
Competitive w/out direct support	17.8	19.3	30.0	52.7	1.8	4.1
Competitive with direct support	0.6	2.4	29.8	21.7	34.9	42.0
Non-competitive but viable in the short run	12.2	20.4	34.5	21.2	63.3	53.9
Noncompetitive and non-viable	69.4	58.0	5.7	4.4	0.0	0.0
TOTAL	100.0	100.0	100.0	100.0	100.0	100.0

Source: Team estimates

132

Possible changes in crop mix or technologies for each of the farm systems are introduced to simulate potential economic incentives after CAP reform. The simulations try to reflect responses to changes in relative profitabilities of the alternative crops and technologies. In some cases, simulated responses involve simple adjustments of farm equipment. In others, changes are more radical, such as increasing the degree of specialization and uprooting permanent crops. For many of the Portuguese systems, these responses are a consequence of public investments in electricity, irrigation and feeder roads. These investments were linked to the Community Structural Framework for 1994-99. Other changes were based on use of the Accompanying Measures of the CAP reform, concerned with the conversion of agricultural land to forest and the expansion of environmentally friendly crop systems.

The potential impact of crop substitution and technical change in the three regions is summarized in Table 6.5. The most obvious implication of the results is that substantial improvements are possible in competitiveness for the Portuguese systems. The prominence of competitive farms increases from 18 to 53 percent of the population; the share of competitive cultivated area increases from 22 to 59 percent. This improvement coincides with a substantial increase in the importance of direct support payments. The improvements often are made possible by complementary private and public investments. For these investments to be widely disseminated in Portugal, large public financial resources must be available. Most of the investments will be feasible only if they are integrated in the structural programs. However, the 1994-99 Regional Development Plan approved for Portugal does not allow for much investment in Northern and Central agriculture.

Competitiveness shows only modest improvement relative to the post-MacSharry baseline in the Italian regions. The improvements in the southern zones reflect further expansion of specialty crops that already have a strong market in Italy. Still, the share of competitive farms increases only from 65 to 68 percent and the area cultivated by competitive farms increases slightly - from 81 to 84 percent. Most small farms are already competitive and most of the obvious public investments in the agricultural sector have been made.

In the hilly rainfed areas, including some of the south and almost all of the central region, problems of non-competitiveness are most apparent. In the central regions, problems arise from inadequate rates of return in agriculture rather than from insufficient total employment. Employment opportunities, either through off-farm work or through full-time farming, appear ample. Systems in the central zone, the area with the highest opportunity cost for labor, have difficulty offering competitive returns in all but the largest farms. Competitive systems in the central region can increase with responses to MacSharry reforms - from 37 to 42 percent of the farms and from 46 to 51 percent of cultivated area. But the gains are small. In the rainfed areas, options for new commodities and new technologies are much more limited than in the other study areas. For small farm agriculture to thrive in rainfed zones, new initiatives must be developed, probably involving research and development

Table 6.5
Italian and Portuguese projected competitiveness, with change

Type of Systems	Northern and Central Portugal		Southern Italy		Central Italy	
	% of No of farms	% of arable land	% of No of farms	% of arable land	% of No of farms	% of arable land
Competitive w/out direct support	22.4	33.2	51.1	73.5	1.8	4.1
Competitive with direct support	30.1	25.4	17.0	10.6	39.7	46.7
Non-competitive but viable in the short run	18.6	21.4	29.6	14.7	58.4	49.2
Noncompetitive and non-viable	29.0	20.0	2.3	1.2	0.0	0.0
TOTAL	100.0	100.0	100.0	100.0	100.0	100.0

Source: Team estimates

134

applications for new commodities, marketing activities, and post-farm systems. Such initiatives have not yet been identified.

Employment from small farms

Small farms must give attention to total employment offered by the farm in addition to rates of return to labor. Farms that can not offer full employment to absorb family labor supplies will be under greatest pressure to change - by increasing farm size, increasing off-farm employment, or both. Pressure to exit agriculture will be most intense where off-farm employment is scarcest; then regional out-migration will be most attractive. Access to off-farm employment is least in some of the interior regions of Portugal and parts of southern Italy. In the latter areas, agriculture accounts for as much as 23 percent of total employment; part-time farms are less common than in the central region. If farms do not offer 'enough' employment, the abandonment of agriculture is expected to be gradual. Studies concur that farms are not quickly responsive to changes in economic circumstances, such as those occasioned by MacSharry. A number of reasons have been suggested for farmers' moderate response, such as asset fixity, the value of the farming lifestyle (including housing), and accessibility to off-farm employment (USDA, 1989; Bryden et al., 1991; OECD, 1994).

The survey data make clear that small farms will not offer much solution to Europe's employment problem (Table 6.6). Small farms provide as much as one FTE for a large share of the population only in southern Italy, a fortuitous result given the lack of off-farm employment in most of the south Italy study areas. Still, just over a third of the south Italy farms offer this much employment. The impacts of changing crop mix and technology ameliorate somewhat this picture of small employment opportunity, particularly in Portugal. But in each of the regions, between 40 and 85 percent of the farms seem destined for part-time status.

Even fewer small farms absorb available family labor. Farms can not absorb family labor available for employment on 37 percent of Portuguese farms, half of southern Italy farms, and three-fourths of central Italian farms (Table 6.6). Irrespective of the rate of return, many small farms are likely to want to increase farm size or off-farm employment. Survey data are consistent with this view, showing that smaller farms have more off-farm employment. In central Italy, for example, 38 percent of Viterbo farms have off-farm employment and farms are usually between 5 and 10 ha. In neighboring Grosseto, farms are often larger than 20 ha, and only four percent have off-farm employment. These results point to the importance of non-agricultural employment policy for the sustainability of small farm agriculture.

Future structural adjustment

Categorization of the systems by potential competitiveness shows the critical role of change for future economic sustainability (Table 6.7). About one-third of the systems (19) will need further changes in crops or technologies to remain

Table 6.6
Employment from the Italian and Portuguese farming systems

Degree of autonomy	Northern and Central Portugal			Southern Italy			Central Italy			Total
	No of systems	% of No of farms	% of arable land	No of systems	% of No of farms	% of arable land	No of systems	% of No of farms	% of arable land	
Type of Systems										
Autonomous ($\geq$ 1 FTE)	18	6.5	20.8	11	37.5	63.1	3	12.1	9.6	32
Potentially autonomous	6	45.2	38.1	7	30.6	21.0	0	0.0	0.0	13
Non-Autonomous	7	48.3	41.1	3	31.9	15.9	7	87.9	90.4	17
TOTAL	31	100.0	100.0	21	100.0	100.0	10	100.0	100.0	62
Absorption of family labor										
Type of Systems										
With capacity of absorption	6	1.6	5.7	3	7.9	21.9	2	1.9	4.1	11
With potential capacity of absorption	18	61.0	64.9	8	44.7	50.1	1	24.0	36.6	27
With no capacity of absorption	7	37.4	29.4	10	47.4	28.0	7	74.1	59.3	24
TOTAL	31	100.0	100.0	21	100.0	100.0	10	100.0	100.0	62

Source: Team estimates

Table 6.7

Classification of the Italian and Portuguese farming systems according to competitiveness

Type of Systems	Northern and Central Portugal			Southern Italy			Central Italy			Total
	No of systems	% of No of farms	% of arable land	No of systems	% of No of farms	% of arable land	No of systems	% of No of farms	% of arable land	
Competitive	11	18.5	23.1	14	59.8	74.4	4	36.7	46.1	29
Potentially Competitive	13	44.1	47.5	4	8.3	9.7	2	4.9	4.7	19
Non-competitive	7	37.4	29.4	3	31.9	15.9	4	58.4	49.2	14
TOTAL	31	100.0	100.0	21	100.0	100.0	10	100.0	100.0	62

Source: Team estimates

137

competitive.   Fourteen of the systems have no potential to attain competitiveness. About half of the systems (29), most of them in Italy, can remain competitive without further change. Potentially competitive systems are particularly important in Portugal (13 of 31), representing 44 percent of farms and 48 percent of cultivated area. These results emphasize again the need in Portugal for technical change and the importance of public and private investment. Change is less urgent in the Italian cases; potentially competitive farms are less than 10 percent of the southern farms and less than 5 percent of the central farms.   In Italy, provision of adequate off-farm employment or increases in size of already profitable systems would appear most critical to the ultimate prominence of small farm agriculture.

Almost all farms are potential participants in structural change. Non-competitive systems will have a structural impact because they will be an important source of supply of land to remaining farmers and a source of labor to the off farm labor market ('an effective structural impact', Table 6.8).   These farms account for nearly half of small farm cultivated area in central Italy and nearly a third of area in the other regions. Some of the farms with a family labor surplus also will leave agriculture, either because they are non-autonomous farms or because the total remuneration to their labor is not sufficient to keep them in agriculture.   Others of these farms will desire to increase farm size or find local off farm employment for some family labor. The third group of farms involved in structural change are the potentially competitive (and competitive) farms able to increase in size. The farms that will want to increase farm size or off farm employment comprise the 'potential structural impact' category and account for at least half of small farm area in each of the regions. This category is especially prominent in Portugal.

Policy for small farm agriculture

Structural change is an inevitable process. Over time, as an economy grows, agriculture becomes a less prominent source of employment.   Economies diversify as incomes increase. But the extent and magnitude of change are not fixed. The particular patterns of structural change and the ultimate role of small farms in the economy are not determinate.   Instead, much depends on cultivation patterns and agro-climatic conditions, the pattern of non-agricultural development, and policy - both agricultural and industrial.

The three regions studied, northwest and central Portugal, southern Italy, and central Italy, represent a wide diversity of small farm environments.   Because they are at very different points in the structural change process, the economic health and policy needs of these areas are different. In the lowest income region (Portugal) needs are 'typical' of a developing agriculture - new technology for agriculture and public investment in rural infrastructure. But in Italy, these investments already have been made.   Together with larger and more consolidated farm structures, much of Italian small farm agriculture already is competitive with other economic activities.   This is particularly true when agronomic and ecological conditions are favorable, such as for the cultivation of horticultural and tree crops. Rainfed, hilly environments for cereal, livestock,

Table 6.8
Classification of the Italian and Portuguese farming systems according to future structural impact

Type of Systems	Northern and Central Portugal			Southern Italy			Central Italy			Total
	No of systems	% of No of farms	% of arable land	No of systems	% of No of farms	% of arable land	No of systems	% of No of farms	% of arable land	Total
With neutral structural impact	0	0.0	0.0	2	6.2	22.0	0	0	0	2
With structural impact	7	37.4	29.4	10	47.4	28.0	4	58.4	49.2	21
With a potential structural impact	24	62.6	70.6	9	46.4	50.0	6	41.6	50.8	39
TOTAL	31	100.0	100.0	21	100.0	100.0	10	100.0	100.0	62

Source: Team estimates

and dairy production present more difficult circumstances. There, full-time farming systems are the more lucrative direction for agriculture. These enterprises may still be 'small' in an economic sense and competitive systems for some of the rainfed areas, such as Ufita, are not apparent from the data presented here. Competitive Viterbo and Grosseto systems are those that offer at least one FTE, 'full time' operations in sheep or dairy production.

Given these characteristics, the MacSharry reforms have little impact on small farms and on the incentives for structural change. The reforms do not much affect the competitive (or non-competitive) status of Portuguese farms. In Italy, returns to many farm systems are reduced, but not enough to affect competitive status. More important is the increase in transparency of policy support. Subsidies to agriculture become explicit, and future demands on the EU budget, perhaps occasioned by economic downturn or further expansion of the Community (Tangermann, 1996), may cause income transfers to be more vulnerable. But for many small farms, MacSharry reforms mean little because much of production concerns commodities outside the traditional realm of EU agricultural policies.

The important policies for small farm agriculture govern access to domestic resources. Access is more important than price. If family labor accepts implicit returns below market wages and costs of production are about the same as those of large farms, small farms should be able to compete economically with larger farms for domestic resources. The key to the success of small farmers is that policy not exclude them from the markets. The large numbers of likely outmigrants and large numbers of farmers who can profitably expand point to the importance of factor market policy, especially land market policy. Labor market policies are important because many competitive farms offer less than one FTE of employment: in south Italy, non-autonomous systems account for 30 percent of arable area; in central Italy, 80 percent of farms are not autonomous; and in Portugal, about half of farms are not autonomous. If these farms are to stay in agriculture, they will need to increase off farm employment or expand farm size.

Capital market access may be less important. In Portugal, the most critical needs involve public investment. Most public investments in Italy have been done; where public investments are limited, they usually are infeasible. An example is central Italy, where irrigation potential is very limited. In Italy, many farms are well-capitalized at present. Claims are common in Viterbo-Grosseto that farms are over-mechanized, with an average of two tractors per crop oriented farm and much underutilized equipment. Utilization rates for machinery also appear low in Basso Molise and other southern regions. But many farms will need to re-capitalize to remain competitive in the future. For example, smaller Viterbo sheep farms have a fragmented farm structure that mandates nomadic milking practices with mobile parlors. This will not be allowed in the new policy for sanitary measures (EC 92/46). These farms need a more consolidated farm structure, implying in turn needs for access to land and capital. Other examples of capital market needs involve changes in technology or crop mix (especially for permanent crops). These require investment and usually access to credit, if off-farm income is not available (as in the south).

140

Market access is particularly critical for Portuguese small farm agriculture, because the magnitudes of change are so great. More than two-thirds of the potentially competitive farms require increases in size (or off farm employment) and changes in technologies and crop mix. For small farms in these regions, flexible factor markets for land, labor, and capital are critical.

Also important are policies that influence the amount and location of complementary public investment and the development of market outlets for permanent crops. The Plano di Desenvolvimento Regional (PDR), designed by the Portuguese government for the 1994-99 period, identifies investments to encourage agricultural change. However, the plans do not allow for much investment in Northern and Central agriculture. The potential absorption of funds in the agricultural sector is about double the level that has been allocated, and the north and center receive only about a tenth of potential demands (Table 6.9). With such limits on public investment, the farms able to introduce successful changes decline drastically, from 44 to 4 percent, and the affected area declines from 48 to 10 percent of the total. Non-competitive systems will comprise more than three- fourths of the farms and two-thirds of the area. Only a few of these farms are likely to be able to finance the simulated changes without access to structural funds.

The policy options to deal with the Portuguese agricultural sector in the event of tight budget constraints depend importantly on the treatment of the land and capital markets, and on the promotion of non-agricultural activities. In this circumstance, policy actions need to facilitate outmigration from agriculture and assist remaining farmers with access to the complementary land and capital resources needed for successful change. Little can be done about helping farmers to get rid of existing capital stocks; these will be gradually depreciated over time. Labor adjustments are not likely to receive much help from agricultural policy because early retirement funds are so small that only a small proportion of exiting farmers can be covered. But useful efforts could be made to complete land registration records and facilitate the free market sale and rental of land. The agriculture that emerges would have a much reduced role for small farms, but it would remain a viable part of the economy.

Southern Italy

Realization of profitable change will require different economic strategies and policy instruments in the studied regions of southern Italy. Introduction of new crops and technologies requires the promotion of market outlets and extension of 'best crop and technology' packages. Movements in farm structure (outmigration of some and expansion of remaining farms) need more flexibility in the land market. The continued survival of many small farms depends on off farm employment opportunities. Industrial policy actions to create alternative sources of off farm income thus become indirectly crucial to the ultimate structure of the agricultural sector.

Agricultural marketing activities are most developed in the Basso Molise-Alta Capitanata regions, but improved efficiency appears possible in all zones.

Table 6.9

Classification of the Northern and Central Portugal farming systems according to budget availability

Type of Systems	Future situation without budget constraint		Future situation with budget constraint	
	% of No of farms	% of arable land	% of No of farms	% of arable land
Competitive	18.5	23.1	18.5	23.1
Potentially competitive	44.1	47.5	3.8	9.8
Non-competitive	37.4	29.4	77.7	67.1
TOTAL	100.0	100.0	100.0	100.0

Source: Team estimates

142

Facilities and capabilities are not adequate to deal with the development of new domestic or external markets and to promote market outlets for new and high quality products. The introduction of new activities and technological improvement of existing activities will require efforts by local research institutions and extension services. However, the selection and extension of new crop and technology alternatives is not sufficient to assure general adoption by farms. Credit access and farmer training will be important components of a policy package to change crops and technologies.

Given the relative profitability of farming in the three southern zones, the greatest problems are expected in Val d'Agri and Ufita-Alta Irpinia. In these two zones, structural adjustment will be difficult because of the lack of off farm employment opportunities. The Basso Molise-Alta Capitanata zone has much stronger off farm employment markets, and this region should have little trouble accommodating changes in the number of farms. The problem farms are primarily those in which the farmers are old or uneducated. For these people, off farm opportunities will be limited, and off farm income alternatives, such as the early retirement program, will take on heightened importance. The early retirement program, introduced by the EC in 1992, could provide incentives for the exit of farmers aged between 55 and 65, making land available to farmers remaining in the sector. At present, funds available for the program amount to almost 1500 billion lira over a 3-year period. About 60 percent of this amount will come from the European Community FEOGA program. The Ministry of Agriculture estimates that the program could apply to 26,500 farms and about 276,000 ha over the 3 years.

Other policies available in the zones originate with the EC. Intervention for on-farm structural adjustment can be made with regulation EC 2328/91. Interventions at the post-farm level can be made under objective 1 of regulation 2052/1988. This regulation can be applied differently in each of the zones, according to specific problems and needs. But so far, the application of regulation 2052/1988 has been limited. Low utilization was due partly to vague definition of the qualifying measures and partly to uncertainty about national financing. Italian use of the funds available under this regulation has been the smallest of all the member states. EC regulations 797/1985 and 2328/1991 had been used very little in the study regions. Between 1986 and 1992, nearly 21,000 farm improvement plans were financed throughout Italy; Puglia and Basilicata accounted for only 334 and 434 of these, respectively, whereas Molise and Campania had no plans. In contrast, the measures that support farm income, such as the compensatory payments for less favored areas and for the mountain zones, were almost universally used.

This result underlines the potential difficulties of implementing policies aimed at efficient development rather than redistribution of income. The preoccupation with subsidies has sometimes precluded farmer access. For example, credit has in the past depended very much on the provision of special subsidy programs. But the transaction costs for application and evaluation have proven onerous, and interest of farmers has waned. Given the magnitude of investment required for a widespread realization of change and the profitability of the simulated changes at the market rates of return to capital, there seems little need to maintain credit subsidies. It is more important to improve access to borrow from financial markets, so that farmers can avoid the constraints of self-finance. Poor access to financial markets will limit the extent and rate of change and result in out-migration from agriculture.

Viterbo and Grosseto

The agricultural changes forecast by the simulation analyses will occur only slowly in central Italy. When fixed costs are considered sunk, total returns are well above the off-farm wage rate for all systems. Non-competitive systems will be expected to disappear from the agricultural sector, but only as capital equipment is depreciated, opportunities arise to sell land resources, and farmers retire from agricultural activity.

Policies will influence the rate and extent of agricultural change. Critical areas for policy are those that affect resource flows into and out of agriculture. Labor market policies and economic development policies are important in affecting the growth and location of off-farm employment. But these policies are largely outside the domain of agricultural policy. More in the domain of agriculture are policies that affect capital and land markets.

Capital market policies focused in the past on the provision of special programs for agriculture. These programs offered the promise of subsidies on interest rates, but the high transaction costs involved in the applications and their evaluation precluded much activity either from farmers or from potential lenders. The simulation analyses indicated that farmers are able to pay the market cost of capital investment. Given the magnitude of investments implied in the largest (profitable) systems, the key factor for farmers will be access to credit markets, not subsidies. Investment requirements implied by growth in livestock herds, purchase of milk quotas, purchase of land, and accommodation to sanitary regulations will be too large for most farmers to meet from their own financial resources, even with income from off-farm employment. A lack of access to financial markets thus will limit the magnitude and rate of agricultural change and encourage out-migration from the agricultural sector.

A second area for policy reform involves land markets. Italian law imposes many controls on the prices and availability of agricultural land for rent or sale. These regulations have been introduced usually with the intention of helping farmers; in practice, they have retarded the exchange of land assets, on either a temporary or permanent basis. But a key change for the competitive farming systems after CAP reform is to increase farm size, either through rental or purchase of land. Small dairies must double their herd size; changes of similar magnitude are necessary to establish profitable sheep systems; some farms will want to consolidate parcels to accommodate the requirements of centralized milking parlors and avoid transportation costs; and increased area is necessary to many crop-oriented farms so that fixed costs can be spread more efficiently.

As in the capital market, the price of the resource is not nearly so important as access to it. The results show that farm systems can afford the market price for land and still compensate labor adequately. The general decline in returns that will follow CAP reform will increase greatly the incentives to sell or rent out land as well as increase the incentives to buy and rent in, and CAP reform has at least the potential to be associated with a very active land market. If the market has many buyers and sellers, the likelihood of price distortion seems small. Rather than attempting to set market prices, policy might serve farmers better by ensuring proper and legitimate contracts between sellers and buyers and between those renting land.

The future for the smallest part-time farms is problematic. Unlike their full-time counterparts, they are not competitive. The mix of commodities currently suited to the hilly, rainfed environments includes cereals, sheep, dairy, and beef, and these are better suited (in economic terms) to full-time operations. In irrigated perimeters near the coast and hazelnut areas, smaller farmers have found a niche as substantial as that in the similar agro-ecological zones of south Italy. But if small farmers are to be able to retain resources in the hilly, rainfed environments, they will need to introduce new commodities, not currently produced there, such as tree crops. These systems are not yet available. Their potential success will depend on substantial programs in research and development and private development of post-farm marketing activities.

Conclusion

Both Italy and Portugal are likely to experience further structural change and outmigration of small farm resources. But the agriculture that will remain in both countries can retain a substantial role for small farms. Particularly where specialty crops and irrigated perimeters are involved, small farms have established a sturdy economic niche. Hilly, rainfed areas present the biggest challenge to attaining a competitive small farm sector, but even there full-time operations are relatively small in terms of farm size and economic dimension.

CAP reform has not altered much the competitive status of the small farm sectors in either country. It has lowered incomes and aggravated problems that already existed or that were caused by inappropriate and unsustainable macroeconomic policies. Reform also has increased the visibility of policy support and thus increased the sector's vulnerability to political changes. Reform thus has heightened the importance of technical change in both countries. The simulated technical changes and crop substitutions in existing farm systems - ranging from minor improvements in efficiency of machinery use to introduction of new crops or uprooting of permanent crops - brought substantial improvement in the prominence of competitive farms in Portugal (to 52 percent of farms and 59 percent of area). Analogous changes had a much smaller impact in Italy - resulting in a modest increase in the proportion of competitive farms, but most farms were able to maintain their competitive status.

Another notable result of the research is the number of farms that cannot become competitive. This share ranges from 30 percent of farms in south Italy to 45 percent of farms in northwest and central Portugal. Structural change thus will be a continuing process. But these manageable magnitudes are dependent on substantial future changes in crop mix, technology, and, particularly in Portugal, public investment. Without these changes, structural changes will be much larger and more difficult to manage. Demand for urban and non-rural area improvements then can be expected to become more strident, and heightened attention will be needed for retraining programs and other traditional solutions to problems of a lagging rural area. The merits and desirability of such directions are now at the center of public debate.

Bibliography

Adams, D. and Graham, D. (1981), 'A Critique of Agricultural Credit Projects and Policies', *Journal of Development Economics* Vol. 8, pp. 347-366.

Bryden, J. et al. (1991), 'Emerging Responses of Farm Households to Structural Change in European Agriculture', unpublished paper, VI European Congress of European Agricultural Economists, Den Haag, Netherlands, September, 1990.

Cioffi, A. and Sorrentino, A. (1997), *La Piccola Azienda e la Nuova Politica Agricola dell'Unione Europea,* Franco Angeli: Milano.

Commission of the European Communities (1982), 'Factors Influencing Tenancy, Ownership, Tenancy, Mobility and Use of Farmland in the Member States of the European Community', *Series Information on Agriculture* No. 86. Office for Official Publications of the European Communities: Luxembourg.

Cory, D., Monke, E.and Jesus, J. (1993), 'Land Markets and Policy', in E. Monke et al., *Structural Change and Small Farm Agriculture in Northwest Portugal,* Cornell University Press: Ithaca, 129-148.

Dono, G., Severini, S. and Sorrentino, A. (1995), 'Constraints to Structural Adjustment of an Extensive Agricultural Area of Central Italy', in F. Sotte (ed.), *The Regional Dimension in Agricultural Economics and Policies,* Ancona, Italy: 40th EAAE Seminar, pp. 275-296.

Folmer, C., Keyzer, M.A., Merbis, M.D., Stolwijk, H.J.J. and Veenendaal, P.J.J. (1995), *The Common Agricultural Policy beyond the MacSharry Reform,* Elsevier Science: Amsterdam.

Gasson, R. (1988), *The Economics of Part-time Farming,* John Wiley: New York.

Iqbal, F. (1986), 'The Demand and Supply of Funds among Agricultural Households in India', in I. Singh, L. Squire, and J. Strauss (eds.), *Agricultural Household Models: Theory and Evidence,* Johns Hopkins University Press: Baltimore, pp. 183-203.

147

Josling, T. and Tangermann, S. (1992), 'MacSharry or Dunkel: Which Plan Reforms the CAP?', Working Paper, International Agricultural Trade Consortium: Minneapolis.

McFadden, D. (1994), 'Contingent Valuation and Social Choice', *American Journal of Agricultural Economics* Vol. 76, pp. 689-708.

Monke, E. et al. (1993), *Structural Change and Small Farm Agriculture in Northwest Portugal*, Cornell University Press: Ithaca.

Portney, P., Hanemann, W. M., Diamond, P. and Hausman, J. (1994), 'Symposia on Contingent Valuation', *Journal of Economic Perspectives* Vol. 8 (Fall), pp. 3-64.

OECD (1990), 'Modelling the Effects of Agricultural Policies', *OECD Economic Studies*, 13.

OECD (1993), *What Future for our Countryside? A Rural Development Policy*, OECD: Paris.

OECD (1994), *Farm Employment and Economic Adjustment in OECD Countries*, OECD: Paris.

OECD (1995), *Adjustment in OECD Agriculture: Issues and Policy Responses*, OECD: Paris.

Saraceno, E. (1994), 'Alternative Readings of Spatial Differentiation: The Rural versus the Local Economy Approach in Italy', *European Review of Agricultural Economics*, Vol. 21, pp. 451-474.

Tangermann, S. (1996), 'Reforming the CAP: A Prerequisite for Eastern Enlargement', Unpublished paper, Kiel Conference on 'Quo Vadis Europe?' Institut fur Weltwirtschaft, Kiel, June, 1996.

USDA (1989), 'Involuntary Exits from Farming: Evidence from Four Studies', *Agricultural Economics Report* No. 625, November.

For Product Safety Concerns and Information please contact our EU
representative GPSR@taylorandfrancis.com Taylor & Francis Verlag GmbH,
Kaufingerstraße 24, 80331 München, Germany

Printed and bound by CPI Group (UK) Ltd, Croydon, CR0 4YY
12/05/2025
01867598-0001